Time & Ego

Judeo-Christian Egotheism
and the
Anglo-Saxon Industrial Revolution

Claudiu A. Secara

ISBN-13: 978-0-9646073-2-3 (trade paper)
ISBN-13: 978-1-892941-39-8 (ebook)

Library of Congress Cataloging-in-Publication Data —

Secara, Claudiu A. (Claudiu Adrian), 1949-
    Time & ego : Judeo-Christian egotheism and Anglo-Saxon Industrial Revolution /
Claudiu A. Secara.
        2nd ed.
        p. cm.
    Includes bibliographical references (p. 111-[115]) and index.
    ISBN 978-0-9646073-2-3 (trade paper: alk. paper) — ISBN 978-1-892941-39-8 (ebook)
1. Duns Scotus, John, ca. 1266-1308. 2. Psychology, Religious—History. 3. Industrial
revolution. I. Title.

    BL53 .S42 1998
    190 21
                            00698325

Printed in the United States

By the same author:

Post-Soviet, Euroslavia

*The New Commonwealth: From Bureau-
cratic Corporatism to Socialist Capitalism*

Table of Contents

< 7 >

1
History as God

1. There are times of solitude and longing when simple *being* bears no wholeness to one's individual existence. Those are times of anguish and anxiety, when the animus alone cannot prevail. In such hours of torment, survival is possible by the will of the genie within—but it is a senseless pursuit since self-preservation is its only purpose.

2. Existential being is the passing away in *blood and flesh,* but history is the reality of living; matter converted into biology, alone, supersedes time—as organic memory. We not only remember yesterday's events but we live as destiny of our past and, as well, as memory of our future.

As spine evolved into mind, we ceased to be biological creatures alone. Consciousness of our double nature, mortal and eternal, emerged out of our awe for *the*

< 11 >

divine. The eternal was extricated from the body and given fantastic existence. The passage of time became an existence in itself. *Becoming* took the name 'God'— history that exists now.

3. It is commonly said that in order to understand the present, one has to look into the past; and it is for this reason that history is taught in schools. In the age of quantum physics, considering time relative to *space, matter, values,* etc. has been reduced to a cliché. However, from a different perspective, time may be seen as the consciousness within which we live. We act consciously relative to a cause and effect relation, which is to say, in relation to time and remembrance.

4. The conviction that there is a constancy and order in the universe gives objective validity to established propositions of knowledge: *"Napoleon died in 1821," "2x2=4."*

The truth as independent of the subject is what positive science aspires to. The relativist interpretations of sophists and dialecticians are possible only as long as their own relativist postulates are thought of as absolutes. Relative to the circumstances, truth is absolute in its determinations: Napoleon died in 1821 relative to our calendar, but, given the calendar, 1821 is the absolute year of Napoleon's death.

Limited by the circumstances of its contingency, one's truth is another's error and the subjective agent is the absolute arbiter. It follows that the subject is the absolute truth.

5. Subjective arbiter par excellence, what man is in his world is what the world is at all. His will and his desires,

< 12 >

his needs and his wants are all that his world is about. His world is the only world, is the whole world, is *the* world. *He* is the world. Ergo, the world is a creation of a free subject. Subjective thought—man's thought—is indeed absolute.

His world is the world of liberty, since it is ruled by his own free will alone. His desires are his only necessities as his will is his only necessity. What he wants is his necessity. Ergo, his liberty is his necessity.

6.   Given his internal necessity, however, man is deprived of the very essence of his external liberty; he is the slave of his own needs. In this sense man's internal nature is revealed to be nature itself. His liberty is nature's liberty. Thus, nature's liberty is his internal necessity, dictating his free will.

Nature acting *within* man is still nature acting in perfect freedom *from* man. The liberty is nature's; the necessity is man's. Man is subservient to his free nature. His nature is transcendent to man and, as such, his own nature is the divine.

7. But man, we know, is a social being. It is mankind, one can say, that is prisoner of social necessity. As an individual, man is still free to determine his own fate. To live or to kill oneself is an individual choice, as is the decision to kill others. As an individual, man has the absolute power of death.

Sovereign over death, man is sovereign over life as well. He is the only being in the universe that procreates other humans. In flesh and blood, he produces mankind. It follows that it is he who originates and incarnates the social being, created and shaped by his demiurgic pow-

< 13 >

ers. Producer of human society, the free individual also originates his own social chains. Social laws and institutions are man's will objectified into the enslavement of society; the social oppressions of the many are the manifestation of each man's freedom.

8. There is a demiurge out there, in every individual, ready to clone into a social multitude of beings. Every individual is a society within itself, capable of reproducing new generations of the social entity. Every individual is the patriarch of his own social constituency that starts with him.

As individuals, humans bring forth other humans. The inception of life takes place day after day and on a mass scale. Each such act is the procreation of individuals by the individual. It is the inbreeding of the subject. Man is the originator of social individuals. That is to say that man creates the social body as well as its structures through the mastery of his creative forces.

In other words, man's sovereignty in generating social bondage is an act of self-determination.

9. Organic reproduction of the human cell, individuals, which is to say, the primordial individual *redivivus*, are the overcoming of time by means of reincarnation, i.e., transcendental mnemonics.

Culture and tradition are forms of collective memory; the sense of identification with the primordial act of birth. *Genesis* is the essence of immortality. The urge to rise up and make our lives last is our deepest longing and that is why, by carrying along the cult of and the respect for our ancestors, we measure our progress and feel comfort and wholeness.

< 14 >

10. Subject to contingent destruction and haphazard perishability, the individual is restored as both personal (specific) and impersonal (immortal) through the social. Blood and flesh, we are the historical first individual. Not just a community of individuals, we are the one primordial individual. We are the historical first man, which is our creator. The original man is within us. And we have a free will of our own because our free will is the original will affirmed in us.

Supreme will and originator, the individual is the social, while community is only the personification of the holistic man.

11. We gain ourselves by carrying on our genealogy. Each individual's parents and their parents and their parents' parents demand the right to live through the individual's personality. There is noise sometimes and quarrel among one's internal voices and it takes deep reflection and self-perception to bring out the internal harmony which is one's own identity.

By contrast, loss of the psychic root is the drama of mental illness, when the question "Who am I?" holds no answer.

12. Harmonizing the inheritance of various inner voices into one individual is the difficult process of maturing through education and self-knowledge. In the end, one finds in his unique being the same pattern of the universal man as everyone else. He is all of his ancestors. We all are only the latest descendant of the first man. Every individual is the first ancestor of the generation to follow.

< 15 >

But who is that one, our first and our common forefather and primogenitor?

In Search of the Ancestor

13. Born out of the bleeding placenta of our incubator, we know where we came from. Our parents themselves came the same way. The tribe one belonged to was set off by the founding father; the great hero and patriarch was the founder of the older nations. Since time immemorial, kinsmen have granted high esteem and godly elevation to the great mythical ancestor. Multiracial nations have created an allegorical father. The most complex civilizations have elaborated a religious father. The West found it in the 'Son of God'.

14. The cult of Christ emerged in the hinterland of Judea at the time of the Roman conquest of Israel.

Encroached and threatened by the new world of Mediterranean cosmopolitanism, Jewish artisans and traders, fishermen and tax collectors were inescapably confronted with living the drama of the estranged local cult of the tribal father. Thus it happened that the people of the chosen tribe living in the internationalized Greco-Roman world were the first to arrive at the heart of the contradiction between the nature of the individual, the tribe and the world.

In the end, in Christ, mankind recognized itself to be one family of one destiny. For the first time, a tribal ancestor

< 16 >

was replaced by the concept of mankind's common salvation.

15. The notion of a unique God, proclaimed first by king Akhnaton in imperial Egypt, emerged after a long process of rationalization of the question of man's destiny. Before it came to be identified with the Biblical notion of a Jewish god, the attributes of the universal fathering Being underwent a long metamorphosis. It finally converged the many gods: from the god of *this* river and the god of *this* tree, to the god of all rivers and the god of all trees. This was already a radical avant-garde accomplishment. In Christ, the notion of a unique creator was now reinforced by the idea of collective responsibility and immortality.

16. By the end of the second millennium BC, an ongoing revolution was taking place in the economies of the river civilizations. With populations expanding incessantly due to the successful cultivation of the riparian lands (Egypt alone grew from 50,000 people in 5000 BC to 6 million by the year 2000 BC), new demands for locally scarce resources and goods rose to unprecedented proportions. Salt, for one thing, and spices and raisins, were unavailable in Egypt. Grain was still plentiful, but Lebanese cedar was much in want in the barren hills of the Nile as well as on the banks of the Euphrates.

Within such an economic environment, the emergence of large-scale trade both required and made possible a new social constituency at the core of the Middle East geographic triangle, bridged through the land of Israel. There, business and the trades took on a life of their own.

Statutes regulating one's occupation, special privileges

< 17 >

in support of specialized work, connections with kinsmen living in far away lands preserved across generations, skills in literacy, mathematics and bookkeeping,
new systems of politics and social interrelations—all
shaped the outlook of that nation's business philosophy.

Eventually, the priestly cast and the engineering corps,
the military elites and the imperial aristocracies, all of
the ancient structures of the surrounding grand riparian
civilizations collapsed. Only business and the trades
moved on along the expanding boundaries of the new
Mediterranean civilization. And so did the idea, initially
developed in collusion with the ancient imperial dynasties' quest for everlasting recognition, of the imperative
of *salvation through the management of time.*

17. That momentous event, the consecration of the
concept and practice of time governing for collective
economic benefit, is preserved to this day in the biblical
story of Joseph.

Within a single generation, from among many similar
tribes—"We are shepherds, sir, just as our ancestors
were,"[1] Jacob introduced his son Joseph to the king of
Egypt—a new household name emerged due only to one
man's new approach to living in time, thinking historically. Joseph advised the king to accumulate grain in
good years—"Take a fifth of the crops during the seven
years of plenty," and "store it up in the cities and guard
it," as a "reserve supply for the country in the seven
years of famine which are going to come on Egypt." He
was right, indeed. The years of famine came but the
future proved to have been surpassed already in the past
and locked out of existence. This holistic perspective on
time brought an unprecedented success to the kingdom
of Egypt as well as to Joseph personally. "Joseph bought

< 18 >

all the land in Egypt for the king. Every Egyptian was forced to sell his land, because the famine was so severe; and all the land became the king's property. Joseph made slaves of the people from one end of Egypt to the other. The only land that he did not buy was the land that belonged to the priests. . . So Joseph made a law for the land of Egypt that one-fifth of the harvest should belong to the king."[2]

The dividend earned by the king paid off his confidence in Joseph and brought Joseph's clan to preeminence as well. "The Israelites lived in Egypt in the region of Goshen, where they became rich and had many children."[3] They "built the cities of Pithom and Ramases to serve as supply centers for the king,"[4] and they became "so numerous and strong that they [were] a threat to [the king]." "In case of war they might join our enemies to fight against us," years later, a new pharaoh feared.

18. In attempting to define the religious content in the story of the old covenant, one finds it more difficult to identify what it *is* rather than what it is not. If one seeks to point to its underlying transcendental theism; if one aims to isolate the supernatural sacred story; if one searches for theological themes and beliefs in divine revelations; if one expects to find the voice of cosmic conscience; if one looks for the worshipping of the mysterious, the unworldly, of the spiritual or the divine; if one probes into the practice of animism, shamanism, idolatry, or divination; if one combs through its messages of theological revelation, theosophy, or the cult of the ancestors; if one examines its teachings of dogmatics, hermeneutics, mystics, hagiographics, revelations, exegesis, or patristics; if the existence of God is to be scrutinized through the religious idea of a metaphysical God, in other words, one cannot find that God in the

< 19 >

story of the Jewish God.

The kingdom of the Judaic God and the pursuit of the Judaic happiness are earthly, ephemeral and godless. "The Lord your God is bringing you into a fertile land—a land that has rivers and springs and underground streams gushing out into the valleys and hills; a land that produces wheat and barley, grapes, figs, pomegranates, olives, and honey. There you will never go hungry or be in need. Its rocks have iron in them, and from its hills you can mine copper. You will have all you want to eat, and you will give thanks to the Lord your God for the fertile land that he has given you."[5] "Then all will go well with you, and you will become a mighty nation and live in that rich and fertile land."[6] "You will lend money to many nations, but you will not have to borrow from any; you will have control over many nations, but no nation will have control over you."[7] "The Lord will give you many children, many cattle, and abundant crops in the land that he promised your ancestors to give you. He will send rain in season from the rich storehouse in the sky and bless all your work, so that you will lend to many nations, but you will not have to borrow from any. The Lord your God will make you the leader among the nations and not a follower, you will always prosper and never fail if you obey faithfully all his commands that I am giving you today. But you must never disobey them in any way, or worship and serve other gods."[8]

In the land of the profane god one must obey the laws and the commands of the profane book of wisdom. And, most of all, one must not worship either gods or idols— that is, not recognize or believe in the sacred nature of any gods!

< 20 >

19. The anti-religious nature of the old covenant, above all, is the rejection of worshipping. For there is nothing out there or up above—no wood, no stone, no light that can be legitimized through acts of worship. God is Cause and Effect, is Law, is Reason, is Time.

It was at this moment in the Middle East's history that the question of moral reasoning (what is good) superseded religious dogmatism (that is idolatry), and practical philosophy superseded the belief in metaphysical worship. "[Reason]—and [Reason] alone—is your God. Love your God [Reason] with all your heart, with all your soul, and with all your strength."[9]

Synthesis of Mesopotamian, Egyptian, Assyrian, Babylonian, Semitic, Persian themes, all coming from within the Middle Eastern cultural paradigm, the Judaic books of wisdom—a mixture of pragmatic philosophies exposed through a series of historical anecdotes, witty fables and prodigy characters in the same vein of folksy theater as the Arabian Nights' story of Noureddin written many years later—hold up thought and reason against superstition and idolatry, consecrating the supremacy of positive knowledge over belief in religious magic.

"You may wonder how you can tell when a prophet's message does not come from the Lord [Reason]. If a prophet speaks in the name of the Lord [Reason] and what he says does not come true, then it is not the Lord's [Reason's] message. That prophet has spoken on his own authority, and you are not to fear him."[10]

Here, one comes as close as possible to positive knowledge and empirical testing. The quest for true knowledge is not so much a religious question as a practical

< 21 >

one (Marx).

20. Scholars who compare the ancient Biblical texts with proven historical data find that the chronologies of the writing and of the events described therein are out of synchronization more often than not. We can surmise, for example, that the book of Genesis was edited ulterior to many of the fundamental texts of the Septuagint, in approximately 500 BC, after the Babylonian captivity and return, because of the heavy infusion of Babylonian mythology.

Absorbing themes from various earlier myths and other sources, recast into a continuous story of one people in pursuit of one aspiration driven by one grand design, the Old Septuagint gives the reader the superior feeling of witnessing the vivid history of the unfolding of a unique plan. The unity of the articulated assemblage of fables, narratives, conjectures and speculations from different times was made possible by one singular and dramatic act: the mystifying covenant with god to worship no god.

True, this epic poem is chronicled in scenic episodes described as matter-of-fact conversations with god— god conferred with Abraham under the "sacred trees of Mamre, as he was sitting at the entrance of his tent during the hottest part of the day"; it spoke with Jacob "beneath the oak tree near Shechem," two hundred years later, and again addressed Moses from behind the flaming bush, some five hundred years later. The impression is overwhelming—it gives the irresistible illusion of both a religious and a historical experience. Yet, the powerful subtext, substance, and nature of the message is instead negative, it is set against previous clan protectors, the snake, the golden calf, even the fire bushes, Baal, or

< 22 >

Ishtar. Those were to be rejected and repudiated in favor of the faceless, the nameless, the impersonal and unique concept of *godlessness and truth.*

We know very little about the time Jacob's descendants spent in Egypt. They arrived as one of the roaming tribes of the Aramaic nation, and they left their country of prosperity, four hundred years from the beginning of their social ascent, as an emancipated nation. Most of all, they rejected by then and left behind the hitherto prevalent and all-inhibiting idols of the mind.

The Egyptians, by their refusal to accept the new teachings, were left captive to obsolete beliefs. Yet, and contrary to its own revolutionary spirit, the insurgent liberation from the idols of reason was being made in the name of a new religion. The negation of religion became a religion in itself.

21. God saying: "Do not worship any gods!"—is atheism in a religious interpretation. The Messiah addressing the crowds: "In the name of god, do not worship or believe in worship!"—is philosophy in popular interpretation.

Christ against Christ

22. As we know, the Laws and the Commandments were the guidebook to the practical God. Where, one might ask, is the divine God? What is the religious way of reaching godly goals, or the divine of one's life? Reading again the book of god, where is god to be found?

< 23 >

In miracles?—True, there were recorded miracles, such as the story of Sarah giving birth at the age of ninety. But the miracle itself is never the point. The point is life on the terrestrial land of fertile Canaan.

In prayer?—True, prayers of glorification and thanksgiving were offered, and solicitous prayers as well. But the prayer itself is never the action and the message. The plot and the drama come from the secular story of the living passions.

In occult pronouncements?—True, there were records of face-to-face encounters with the divine. Yet these personal encounters were never occult; everyone had to know about the matters being discussed with the heavenly messenger, they were expressed openly in public squares for the entire community's benefit, read aloud to the crowds.

In power emanating from the high clergy?—True, the Old Testament is full of prophets and seers. They were the central leaders of the Judaic intellectual class, yet none of them was part of a religious establishment; neither were they priests, shamans, rabbis, or sacerdotal high clerics, theologians or spiritual princes. There was no practice of magic, no incantations, occult rites, necromancy or thaumaturgy, no astrology, hypnotism or witchcraft, no fetishism, spiritualism, black art or mystic rituals. No transcendentally or supernaturally possessed individuals were central figures— just simple folk with a commonsense wisdom.

Artisans in the understanding of human psychology, rather than masters; moralist novelists and writers of historical drama, they brought poetry and story telling,

< 24 >

fiction and allegory, parable and character description, the art of literature, in other words, to the level of moral philosophy. Poetic characters made social science with artistic means.

"Poetic characters," in the words of Giambattista Vico— the essence of the "Heroic Age" stories— appeared "out of the need of human nature to explain itself while still incapable of isolating the forms and the attributes of things through the act of abstraction."[11] "There is a certain feature (says Vico) of primitive nations, namely, that they don't know how to advance from concrete to abstract. Unlearned of how to abstract the general attributes out of concrete objects, they would rather indicate the latter and thereby the former, that is, the attributes themselves through the respective objects. The Latin grammars contain many examples."[12] And then further: "One can say that in legends and fables, nations have, crudely, described the principles of this world of science; and, helped by rationalization as well as by maxims, that crude world of science has been rendered intelligible by the reflective thought of learned men." *"...The poetic theologians were the senses, while the philosophers were the intellect of human wisdom."*[13]

23. The high brow revolutionary poly-atheism [a-polytheism] (the rejection of supernatural powers) soon became ego-theism—worship of One, oneself. The intellectual dimension of non-religious higher philosophical understanding has been corrupted into a new religion of monotheistic self-worship. God as deity was now the chosen people as god.

This new religion made out of anti-superstition a superstition in itself and a fully developed institution of worship was created and cultivated.

< 25 >

A well-established class of servants of the forbidden gods, as well as entrenched special interests, made empty phrases out of the revolutionary teachings. Priests, Sadducees, Pharisees, Teachers all busily debated the nature and the validity of the new rules. Worship of the secular reached its paroxysm. The un-worldly spirit made a full religion out of the worldly.

Now, interpretations of the un-interpretable functioned as the equivalent superstitious belief in the pagan interrogations of the auguries. Long successions of fortunetellers and false prophets came to populate the land of the latest god. Public displays and rituals stood out as the practices of a new-style faith while literal interpretations of the sacrosanct texts would obscure both their meaning and their spirit.

It was about time for a second revolution.

24. "Do not think that I have come to do away with the Law of Moses and the teachings of the prophets. I have not come to do away with them but to make their teachings come true."[14] A new hero stood up, for a moment, to the newer religious bureaucratic establishment. The "heroic character", once again, brought the principles of rational philosophy and ethical life to the forefront of human consciousness. Jesus articulated an anti-religious position and a humanistic manifesto. He, too, would be sacramentalized and idolatrized while still alive, and after a martyr's death.

25. Ambitious men have a shared, sometimes hidden, desire for fame and glory.

Fathering new teachings on god and his designs on earth

< 26 >

always seems to fascinate the great dreamers and more than one life has been spent on such pursuits. Would-be founders of new religions act out their own belief in religious engineering. Many still believe that mass conversions to virtually any form of superstition are possible. In that case, having at hand a great communicator of popular simple-minded prejudices, backed up by astute crowd hypnotism and an organization to spread the last word of wisdom, making up some newspaper story of persecutions, an occasional fabricated martyr— and a new religion product could be thought out as designer made by any ingenious entrepreneur.

Yet, as long as the aim of creating a religion is a religious one, the result is only "religious". The true religions were, at their very core, anti-religious movements. The true religions were indeed atheistic.

Christ was second after Moses, in our tradition, to rise up in a fundamental way against the fetish spirit, the spirit which nurtures only religious monsters.

Humanism as Religion

26. In the panoply of man's teachers, Christ had an unparalleled influence. Why is that? What makes the story about him so unique? What is Christ's overriding message, what is the essential message of the New Testament, its central idea? Is it the teachings of Christ, and if so which ones? Or, is it what is implied by the deeds of Christ, and if so, once again, which ones? Is the

< 27 >

symbol of Christ, as a mythical figure, the message, and then, what does his symbol represent?

There are at least three major levels of communication embedded in the writings of the New Testament, skillfully melded into one story yet strikingly distinct from each other. One story comes from third party witnesses and their story *about* Christ. The second story is in his *actions:* healing the terminally ill, multiplying the loaves of bread, walking on water—still not unlike some traditional exorcist and occult magician. The third story is Christ's own *words*— his parables, teachings, lessons.

On the first level and by all accounts, what is known as Christ's divine nature—his birth and death, and especially his resurrection—is related to us by later writers in the *Gospels.* These myth-tellers were not historians in any sense. As embodiment of a myth, Christ is what he has been made to be.

On the second level of interpretation, there are ways to rationalize and make sense of his acts of miracles only when interpreted as *"concrete* descriptions" of some *"poetic intellectual thinking,"* which brings us to the third level of Gospel exegesis.

It is what Christ says that has the most insightful historical value, because what he tells his fellow men is a meaningful extension of the Hebrew spirit of his times, good Hellenistic philosophy, and free-thinking, all blended together into one new set of principles. "They teach man-made rules as though they were my laws! You put aside God's commands and obey the teachings of men,"[15] he quotes Isaiah,[16] and few in his audience seem to understand the basis of his rejection of his fellow countrymen's uncritical belief in old ideas.

< 28 >

Socrates announcing the death of the tribal idols and subjective falsehood is the closest figure, in antiquity, to that of Christ.

'What is the most important commandment of all?' he is asked. His answer as recorded by his chroniclers is: "The Lord our God is the only Lord. Love the Lord your God with all your heart, with all your soul, with all your mind, and with all your strength."[16]

27. One needs only to read his words through the eyes of modern social science to capture the revolutionary sense of this proposition. The concept of *objective truth* is outright seditious incitement to self-liberation from fallacy, mendacity, and human vanity. It is anti-establishment.

Here, the concept of god is like the concept of order and law, objective knowledge and science, as opposed to falsehood, irrationality, superstition, and ignorance. *There is a natural order in this world*—is the underlying message. The law of the universe is the law of nature, of existence, the law of being. True thinking is love of the whole truth, of the universal truth. Only religion is idolatry of self, belief in man-made, self-made fetishes, in subjective truths.

God is omniscient, omnipresent, all-powerful—the reason in things. Metaphorical philosophy—nature explained through the act of nature itself—Christ's intellectual discourse takes the form of poetic fables. Notice that he has not a single word on the matter of the attributes of some supernatural reality. Knowledge and understanding of things and belief in oneself are the proof of the mastery of the powers of mind. Seek and you will find, believe and you will be powerful. And

< 29 >

above all—know thyself.

28. The pedantic mind, prisoner of his own fetishes, sees only opposites: soul or body, spirit or matter, science or religion. In fact, in presenting the notion of a unifying supreme being, Christ makes no distinction between the sides of our existence, soul and heart, spirit and body, will power and love—they are equally invoked as ways of acknowledging the laws of the universal being.

29. One basic tenet of modern dialectical materialism is the enunciation of the unity of opposites as in the identity of *one into another.* A more complex understanding of the dialectical philosophy of nature is given by the natural law of the identity of *one into many.* A still higher understanding is the notion of metamorphosis, transformation and evolution: *one of many.*

Identity in diversity is recognized as the underlying premise in any universal judgment such as when one announces that *all swans are white (all A are B).* The general attributes of things (*white,* in this case) have identical existence and it is easy to believe that they might also have real existence outside and independent of the things themselves. The color *white* is an attribute independent of any particular swan so that one can unintentionally fall on the slippery conviction that it can be extrapolated into an independent existence. Hence the scholastic assertion that *universalia sunt realia.*

The philosophical notion of *becoming* is magic explanation of how *A* transforms into *B.* Metamorphosis takes place in Time. Time is a three dimensional perspective of a flat world. Circular *becoming* is the negation of negation. The spiral of becoming is the negation of circular becoming. One seed grows into a mature plant which

< 30 >

carries the many seeds of its fruition. The real thing is neither the seed not the plant, it is the process of transformation, the process of becoming the other one. The real thing is an abstraction. *Things are really processes.* Hence: *Nomina sunt realia.* What is real is a description.

The model of the *living being* illustrates best the dialectics of transformation. Things are living organisms. The Earth is Gaia. The universe is a Spirochete. The whole is a symbiosis of the larger infinite Being into the smaller infinity of beings (Nicholas Cusanus). Parts of the whole, they are living wholes unto themselves.

For the nineteenth century philosophy of dialectics, the concept of *unity in contradiction* was the representation of a simplified bipolar model of nature: the magnetic unity of positive and negative. It was a dialectical philosophy of the electrical age. Life as assimilation and disassimilation, society as master and slave, knowledge as science and religion.

A bipolar dialectic, however, is only one particular slant on the multifaceted philosophy of dialectics.

30. The idea that soul is body, that spirit is matter, or that science is religion is still not above the bipolar notion of dialectics. The opposite idea, that religion is science, is no less traditional dialectics. Yet, understanding that *atheism is religion* also, or that religion—the uncritical belief in subjective metaphysical constructs—is the very basis of our intellectual rational assertions, is taking dialectical philosophy one step further.

31. Modern exegesis of the history of religions brought to larger circulation the view that scientific novelty and

< 31 >

advancement in knowledge becomes, in the course of time, outdated representation. Science becomes religion as dead science. Or, science becomes religion for ignorant, non-scientific minds.

Nevertheless, the view that science itself is theism—that is, belief in objective absolute causes; as much as theism is atheism—that is the rejection of subordination to an external authority; that religion is fetishism—namely that one's scientific premises are his idols; that idolatry is the affirmation of one's individuality—as in the belief in the subjective power of knowledge, etc., has unexpected consequences.

32. We still tend to make judgments based on semantic assumptions, words as thought realities, not unlike old scholasticism. The French Revolution, for instance, was argued in the anti-feudal concepts of human rights, as the Russian Revolution was worded through anti-capitalist notions of labor power. The use of terms such as *human rights* or *proletarian power,* reflected in the lexicography of the time, misses the universality of the human drama. Prometheus against Zeus, David against Goliath could as well be thought of as human rights movements, or proletarian movements. They asserted their human rights and they rebelled against social enslavement, against fear and idolatry. They stand as symbols of the eternal struggle of the underdog against the authority, of sons against fathers, of God against Devil.

Yet, by the logic of revolution itself, it follows that the underdog turns into the new authority, son turns into father, God turns into Devil. We have now a continuation of the same antagonism, only the terms have changed: authority against the underdog, fathers against

< 32 >

sons, Devil against God. God turned into Devil. God is Devil. God himself is godless.

This is a plot in a myriad of plots that plot. God is everywhere. God is godless. Godlessness is godly.

33. Philosophically, Christ is the iconoclastic god and as such he is godless. Center and kernel of the power that emanates from him, he is the father, Alpha and Omega, the One and the negation of the Other. *He is atheist because he is the divine.* He is divine because he is the unique One. We are all unique, ergo we all are Christ.

34. Historically, Christ is the individual that came from within Judaism's philosophical religion and impressed his countrymen with his teaching of submission to no religious authority. They were in awe, expecting a polit-ical Messiah, but they were confronted with Jesus' own anti-Christ spirit—ancient interpretation of what modern-day philosophy has more elaborately defined as dialectical materialism.

35. Throughout the Gospels, there is a strikingly recog-nizable story in the struggles of the courageous man confronting old habits, hypocrisy, plain stupidity, pow-erful economic influences, entrenched interests, even the house of worship's self-appointed men (later-on, sadly, reenacted in his own name).

Listen to the story of his poetical philosophy:

36. Man, his life, his needs, his self-interest, should be recognized as the central issue for man:

"The Sabbath was made for the good of man; man was not made for the Sabbath. So the Son of Man is Lord even

< 33 >

of the Sabbath." *Mark 2, 27-28.*

"What does our Law allow us to do on the Sabbath? To help or to harm? To save a man's life or to destroy it?" *Mark 3,4.*

> The standpoint of the old materialism is *"civil"* society; the standpoint of the new is *human* society, or socialized humanity. *Marx, Theses on Feuerbach, X.*

37. Natural laws govern the objective world, independent and outside of man's subjective thinking.

"The Kingdom of God is like this. A man scatters seed in his field. He sleeps at night, is up and about during the day, and all the while the seeds are sprouting and growing. Yet he does not know how it happens. The soil itself makes the plants grow and bear fruit: first the tender stalk appears, then the head, and finally the head full of grains. When the grain is ripe, the man starts cutting it with his sickle, because harvest time has come." *Mark 4,26-29.*

"What shall we say the Kingdom of God is like? What parable shall we use to explain it?. . . A man takes a mustard seed, the smallest seed in the world, and plants it in the ground. After a while it grows up and becomes the biggest of all plants. It puts out such large branches that the birds come and make their nests in its shade." *Mark 4,30-32.*

> The question whether objective truth can be attributed to human thinking is not a question of theory but is a *practical* question. Man must prove the truth, that is, the reality and power, the this-sidedness of his thinking in practice. The dispute over the reality or non-reality of

< 34 >

thinking which is isolated from practice is a purely *scholastic* question. *Marx, Theses on Feuerbach, II.*

38. Believing in one's self is believing in man's creative forces in an intellectual as well as practical way:

"He would not speak to them without using parables, but when he was alone with his disciples, he would explain everything to them." *Mark 4,34.*

"My daughter, your faith has made you well." *Mark 5,34.*

"Don't be afraid, only believe." *Mark 5,36.*

"He was not able to perform any miracle there, except that he placed his hand on a few sick people and healed them. He was greatly surprised, because the people did not have faith." *Mark 6, 5-6.*

"Have faith in God. I assure you that whoever tells this hill to set up and throw itself in the sea and does not doubt in his heart, but believes that what he says will happen, it will be done for him. For this reason I tell you: when you pray and ask for something, believe that you have received it, and you will be given whatever you ask for." *Mark 4,22-24.*

> Feuerbach wants sensuous objects, really distinct from the thought objects, but he does not conceive human activity as *objective* activity.[. . .] Hence he does not grasp the significance of "revolutionary," of practical-critical, activity. *Marx, Theses on Feuerbach, I.*

39. Knowledge is empirical perception of things, seeing and listening, and is the intelligent, logical and rational

< 35 >

use of mind powers:

"You are no more intelligent than the others. Don't you understand? Nothing that goes into a person from the outside can really make him unclean, because it does not get into his heart but into his stomach and then goes on out of the body." *Mark 7,18-19.*

"For from the inside, from a person's heart, come the evil ideas which lead him to do immoral things, to rob, kill, commit adultery, be greedy, and all sorts of evil things; deceit, indecency, jealousy, slander, pride, and folly—all these evil things come from inside a person and make him unclean." *Mark 7, 21-23.*

" 'Take care and be on your guard against the yeast of the Pharisees and the yeast of Herod.' They started discussing among themselves: 'He says that because we don't have any bread.' Jesus knew what they were saying, so he asked them: 'Why are you discussing about not having any bread? Don't you know or understand yet? Are your minds so dull? You have eyes— can't you see? You have ears— can't you hear?' " *Mark 8, 14-18.*

"The disciples were completely amazed, because they had not understood the real meaning of the feeding of the five thousand; their minds could not grasp it." *Mark 6,51.*

> Social life is essentially *practical*. All mysteries which mislead theory into mysticism find their rational solution in human practice and in the comprehension of this practice. *Marx, Theses on Feuerbach, VIII.*

40. The universal character and validity of true knowledge proves the unity of nature and its laws:

< 36 >

"Whoever welcomes in my name one of these children, welcomes me; and whoever welcomes me, welcomes not only me but also the one who sent me." *Mark 9,37.*

"Whoever listens to you listens to me; whoever rejects you rejects me, and whoever rejects me rejects the one who sent me." *Luke 10,16.*

"As Jesus was walking in the Temple, the chief priests, the teachers of the Law, and the elders came to him and asked him: 'What right do you have to do those things? Who gave you such right?' Jesus answered them: 'I will ask you just one question, and if you give me an answer, I will tell you what right I have to do these things. Tell me, where did John's right to baptize came from: was it from God or from man?' " *Mark 11,27-30.*

> Feuerbach, consequently, does not see that the "religious sentiment" is itself a social product, and that the abstract individual whom he analyses belongs in reality to a particular form of society. *Marx, Theses on Feuerbach, VII.*

41. The preeminence of the Godly truth is to be understood as the preeminence of the objective truth over the ideas of socially dominant classes' truth and their vested class interests and false ideologies.

"Teacher, we know that you tell the truth without worrying about what people think. You pay no attention to a man's status but teach the truth about God's will for man." *Mark 12,14.*

"When they arrived in Jerusalem, Jesus went to the Temple and began to drive out all those who were

< 37 >

buying and selling. He overturned the tables of the moneychangers and the stools of those who sold pigeons, and he would not let anyone carry anything through the Temple courtyards. He then taught the people: 'It is written in the Scriptures that God said, 'My Temple will be called a house of prayer for the people of all nations.' But you have turned it into a hideout for thieves!' The chief priests and the teachers of the Law heard of this, so they began looking for some way to kill Jesus. They were afraid of him, because the whole crowd was amazed at his teaching." *Mark 11,15-18.*

> The philosophers have only *interpreted* the world, in various ways; the point, however, is to change it. *Marx, Theses on Feuerbach, XI.*

42. Learning and acquiring knowledge is an ongoing process, it is keeping up with the times and historical change, with the evolution of society, it is answering one's own social challenges, dealing with the reality of the historical present time and not worshipping of the past:

"Now, as for the dead being raised: haven't you ever read in the Book of Moses the passage about the burning bush? There it is written that God said to Moses, "I am the God of Abraham, the God of Isaac, and the God of Jacob.' He is the God of the living, not of the dead. You are completely wrong!" *Mark 12,26-27.*

> Feuerbach resolves the religious essence into the human essence. But the human essence is no abstraction inherent in each single individual. In its reality it is the ensemble of the social relations.
>
> Feuerbach, who does not enter upon a criticism of this real essence, is consequently compelled:

< 38 >

(1) To abstract from historical process and to fix the religious sentiment as something by itself and to presuppose an abstract—*isolated*—human individual.

(2) The human essence, therefore, can with him be comprehended only as "genus," as an internal, dumb generality which merely *naturally* unites the many individuals. *Marx, Theses on Feuerbach, VI.*

43. The word, law, universal and objective Reason, is God and it is not observed or attended to by religious rituals but by following the commandments of living rationally:

"Well done, teacher! It is true, as you say, that only the Lord *is* God and that there is no other god but he. It is more important to obey these two commandments than to offer on the altar animals and other sacrifices to God." *Mark 12,32-33.*

"Teachers of the Law, who like to walk around in their long robes and be greeted with respect in the marketplace, who choose the reserved seats in the synagogues and the best places at feasts. . . they take advantage of widows and rob them of their homes, [they] teach men [to] swear by the gold in Temple, [to] swear by the gift on the altar. . . You hypocrites! You give to God one tenth even of the seasoning herbs, such as mint, dill and cumin, but you neglect to obey the really important teachings of the Law, such as justice and mercy and honesty." *Matthew 23,16-23.*

The materialist doctrine that men are products of circumstances and upbringing [. . .] forgets that it is men who change circumstances and that it is essential to educate the educator himself. Hence, this doctrine necessarily arrives at dividing society into two parts, one of

< 39 >

which is superior to society.

The coincidence of the changing circumstances and of human activity can be conceived and rationally under-stood only as revolutionizing practice. *Marx, Theses on Feuerbach, III.*

44. The proof for knowledge is sought in a practical way by experimental methods and it is not an abstract or untested imitation of affected scientific manners:

"You may wonder how you can tell when a prophet's message does not come from the Lord [Reason]. If a prophet speaks in the name of the Lord [Reason] and what he says does not come true, then it is not the Lord's [Reason's] message. That prophet has spoken on his own authority, and you are not to fear him."[10]

"Teacher, we saw a man who was driving out demons in your name, and we told him to stop, because he doesn't belong to our group." *Mark 9,38.*

"For false Messiahs and false prophets will appear. They will perform miracles and wonders in order to deceive even God's chosen people, if possible." *Mark 13,22.*

Feuerbach, not satisfied with *abstract thinking*, appeals to. *sensuous contemplation;* but he does not conceive sensuousness as practical, human-sensuous activity. *Marx, Theses on Feuerbach, V.*

45. Knowledge is reason, reason is divine power, is godly and so is the man who exercises knowledge in the eyes of the ones who don't have it:

"Again the High Priest spoke to him, 'In the name of the living God I now put you under oath: tell us you are the

Messiah, the Son of God.' Jesus answered him: 'So you say.'" *Matthew 26:64.*

"They all said, 'Are you, then, the Son of God?' He answered them, 'You say that I am.'" *Luke 22:70.*

> Feuerbach starts out from the fact of religious self-alienation, of the duplication of the world into a religious, imaginary world and a real one. [...] For the fact that the secular basis detaches itself from itself and establishes itself in the clouds as an independent realm can only be explained by the cleavage and the self-contradictions within this secular basis. *Marx, Theses on Feuerbach, IV.*

46. The question of truth is the question of being human. For man, only truth has reality and power:

"You say that I am a king. I was born and came into the world for this one purpose, to speak about the truth. Whoever belongs to the truth listens to me." *John 18:37.*

> Man must prove the truth, that is, the reality and power, the this-sidedness of his thinking in practice. *Marx, Theses on Feuerbach, II.*

47. The question of truth? With this question the metaphysical Eastern religion arrives at the gates of Western philosophy; Greco-Roman rational philosophy takes notice for the first time, as recorded by written history, of the poetic Jewish mind. The rational-skeptical Pilate finds the issues that strain his learned prisoner's mind to be familiar and yet still approached with a naive dogmatism. He looks down upon the young true believer from his own nation's centuries-old rational wrestlings with the metaphysics of truth:

< 41 >

" 'And what is truth?' Pilate asked." *John 18:38.*

With that we enter the poetical Middle Ages.

48. Christ spoke to the people in his audience about themselves and their earthly existence, and they conjured him up as an unearthly creature. He pinned them to the wall of shame and mocked their endless foolishness, and they fell deeper into their mindless self-righteousness. He deplored their inner wickedness and hypocrisy, and they condemned him for apostasy and heresy. He challenged them to think; they prayed and pleaded for their salvation in the name of their self-interest.

49. A remarkable common-sense view of nature, life and truth strikes the unencumbered mind when it reads with an open eye the desperate effort of that man to tell his people how to live with an intelligent approach to their destiny on earth. They took a literal interpretation of his subtle spirit of dialectical thinking and entirely obscured his message.

He spoke in allegories about the powers of the mind and man mastering nature's elements, its forces and demons; and his people swore they saw him one day walking the seas. He pointed to the hill above the plain, domesticated and developed under the tending hand of man, and they swore he had ordered the hill tumble off the reef. He spoke in parables, and they looked for fantastic apparitions.

He told them that spreading the wisdom of understanding is like the yeast that makes the dough grow from within itself, and they said he fed thousands of stomachs with one loaf of whole grain bread.

< 42 >

He cited the miraculous in the quotidian, the miraculous found in the seed of the germinating grain, in the grass sprouting from the earth's crust, in the unfolding of the mustard tree, in the lilies flowering in the fields, in the wind and the rain, in all the wonders of the Kingdom of Life, and they were concerned with how to reserve a place in the Kingdom of death.

He asked them to see and to hear and they beheld him in disbelief and were disturbed by hearing their own inner voices and outer whispers of condemnation.

He saw liberation from the chains of greed, deceit and jealousy through self-restraint and dignity—and they sought, behind the words of truth, some sort of hidden insiders' message of better terms on their life's transaction.

He said, don't ask whether the truth comes from God or from man, the question itself is silly since man is the son of God, man is a product of nature. They questioned man's freedom to question.

He told them that performing miracles is not proof of truth, anybody astute enough can learn that skill; and they founded his supernatural ontology on the art of magic and deceit.

He lived in flesh and blood on the streets of the cities and walked the roads and the fields of Judea, and they made him an unearthly abnormality.

He was teaching modern science; they worshiped a spectral creation of feverish minds.

< 43 >

50. One Gospel or another, one story more or less, the generations followed, all mixing truth with falsehood in such a way that verity and religion, idols and heroes, high aspirations and fallacies would establish their patterns under new names. And a good cause was defended for the wrong reasons.

< 44 >

2
Atheist Monotheism

51. Between the view that attacks Christian religion as mental opiate and the view that regards it as a divine message, there is the historical view, which is concerned with Jewish society and its development in contact with the synergetic and cosmopolitan Rome.

Cultural ambiguities and mystical frenzies, experimentation with a pandemonium of beliefs, ethnic agglomerations, races and crazes, all convened into the Roman metropolis of hopelessness. — In this sense, they are paralleled only by the blighted American ethnic inner-cities at the end of the second millennium AD.

Philosophical sects and fraternities celebrating the mysteries of the Orient proclaimed themselves saviors from death; pious feasts glorified minor founders as great

< 47 >

heroes, hymns and ceremonies assumed the semblance of a spiritual revival; liturgy and piety, divination and prophesy guaranteed the blessing of eternal happiness. Rites of purification, astrological fortunetelling and henotheistic initiation, mysteries and practices of self-mortification, magic mongering, channelling spirits, dream reading and haruspex soothsaying—they offered the latest answer to all questions and a respite from worldly anxieties. They held the explanation of the world, the rules of conduct, the release from evil and from death.

Reprocessed through the schools of Hellenistic higher interpretations and packaging, such intellectual products of the East were converted into Roman gods, molded into new images under the pressure of Rome's spiritual vacuum and lack of cohesive values.

Still long after the conquests of Alexander, the gods of the Orient continued to cross into the fringes as well as further deep into the very heart of continental Europe as spiritual fantasies—devoid of deep roots, removed from their own native soil, having no inner developed patterns of life, and offering only exotic mythologies and symbolisms as one more elixir for the already over-imbued Roman spiritual consumer:

Attis at Ostia, reinforced by the decrees of Claudius; Cybele, the Great Idaean Mother of the Gods (whose cult was celebrated in the Palatine since 191 BC, the liturgy reformed by the same Claudius); Isis and Serapis, whose temple, destroyed by fire in 80 AD, was rebuilt by Domitian; Hadad and his consort Atargatis (Dea Syra) had their temple in Rome where Nero, who denied all other gods, granted homage; Mithra had well-established temples in Rome and Capua as had the cult of the Baalim.

< 48 >

Those few Romans who stood cool-minded in the face of this spiritual invasion did suspect the opiate effects on their fellow citizens. Juvenal, the satirist, charges them with charlatanism regardless of their origins, be they Chaldean, Commagenian, Phrygian or Egyptian. His description may disregard the sincerity and the honest naivete of many of the new converts, but it gives a good sense of the spiritual impoverishment of the faithful. Here is his portrait of the mysteries of 'Bona Dea, the Good Goddess': "when the flute stirs the loins and the Maenads of Priapus sweep along, frenzied alike by the horn blowing and the wine, whirling their locks and howling. What foul longings burn within their breasts! What cries they utter as the passion beats within!" Or, see the procession of the priest of Isis, "who with his linen-clad and shaven crew runs through the streets under the mask of Anubis and mocks at the weeping of the people." One woman "in the winter will go down to the river, in a morning, break the ice, and plunge three times into the Tiber," then, "naked and shivering she will creep on bleeding knees right across the field of Tarquin the Proud." Another, "at the command of White Io will journey to the confines of Egypt and fetch water from hot Meroe with which to sprinkle the Temple of Isis." Or, one could have seen, as did Seneca, men laughing in the streets of Rome as they hurled themselves head-on into the rolling spokes of a passing carriage.

And over all this seizure of carnal carnival and lunacy that overtook the souls and bodies of the once virtuous Roman, an even stranger sort of cult and belief was making its appearance: the sect of the Christians.

52. The existence of the Jewish colony in Rome dates from the beginning of the Empire, and its presence was

< 49 >

only consecrated through the goodwill of Julius Caesar,[1] in 44 AD. The size of the colony is attested by the fact that 4,000 Jews, relocated to Sardinia in 19 AD by Tiberius, were known to be only a small segment of a larger community. The first Christians from Jerusalem penetrated Rome, breaching the unity of the Jewish colony first, clashing with the upholders of the ancient Mosaic law, and then clashing with the champions of the other ancient faiths.

53. Ever since, one question has haunted the critical Western mind. Why Christianity? What was the special element that made this religion more attractive than any other? Why were its heavy doses of supernatural fallacy more convincing than other beliefs of the time? Why did its absurd and eccentric tenets, the immaculate birth, resurrection from death, etc., originally sanctioned by the state chancellery as collective alienation and mental derangement, later on prove to be so irresistibly appealing to all walks of life, from rich to poor, from the sophisticated to the ignorant, nations and races alike? How could such a belief become so widespread against the commonsense wisdom and dispensing with the self-doubting questioning of the evidence on matters of truth?

54. One way to explore this intriguing puzzle is to make an inventory of the mythical poetic rationality of Christian religion, an approach that will give Christian thinking a high level of rationality compared to other religions.

Many common themes of mythical character, about life and death, regeneration of vegetation, the cycle of nature, the immortality of the universe, etc., are easy to identify, all responding to the experience and the spiri-

< 50 >

tual needs of the agrarian nations. Sowing and harvesting, the cycles of spring and fall, the succession of the generations and so on, all are elements of Christian symbolism as they are inextricably woven into its ancient semantics which, indeed, were far from the absurd literal interpretations of the theologians and the dogmatics of the later times.

Similar cults were followed long before and have been preserved in small communities even now. The cult of Mithra or Attis are two examples of the same myth of resurrection found in different nations and, indeed, functioning in response to the same needs. Like Isis, who stands for the Christian Virgin Mother, or the Sea, now Mary Magdalene, many other formerly autonomous ritual-driven gods can be uncovered from under the synergetic story of the quintessentially psychopathic myth of the resurrected Christ.

In this sense, Christianity offers only a representation of the highest level of abstraction in which all the elements of agrarian myths from around the Mediterranean world were lumped together into one myth.

This is the mythological explanation of the origin and functionality of the Gospel of Christ and it is, indeed, of great value—except for one persistent shortcoming. Why did such a myth develop in the far land of Judea and what ingredient of the non-mythical Jesus proved to be so decisive, so essential in his original human story that it became the very foundation of a later construct? Christ, as we know him from the Gospels, is a fully developed mythological character, certainly a religious product by now. Under the layers of ulterior sediments accrued by later authors, what was so compelling in the reality of the historical Joshua?

< 51 >

55. From the experience of modern nations, more so than ever before, one sees, in a class warfare sense, that a social cause appeals to the masses—even bordering on collective frenzy—only when calls to action bring changes in the real life of those people.

Social action, political activism, clearly perceived economic emancipation on a wide social scale, mobilizes unreserved popular support. Napoleon, Garibaldi, Marx, Lenin, Mao, Che Guevara, Ayatollah Khomeini command veneration from their millions of followers due to the expected impact on their lives.

But what real changes might Jesus have brought to his followers, if any?

56. There are two essential elements that set Jesus Christ apart from any of the other mythical heroes of the time. One is that he came from within the Judaic cultural tradition. The other is that he was a radical reformer of that very system.

Judaism was already far ahead of other cultures in the radicalism of its social consciousness. Yet, a still deeper reform was making the reform itself into a revolution.

Judaism as an Economic Culture

57. One distinctive feature of the Jewish political and economic system is that it is a community of free indi-

< 52 >

viduals. At a time when slavery was the main source of manpower throughout the Middle Eastern societies, from Imperial Egypt to the rigidly stratified India, the Jews' known social/juridical system was endorsed and preserved by that ancient Judaic constitution, the Law and the Commandments.

> Give the Israelites the following laws: If you buy a Hebrew slave, he shall serve you for six years. In the seventh year he is to be set free without having to pay anything. If he was unmarried when he became your slave, he is not to take a wife with him when he leaves; but if he was married when he became your slave, he may take his wife with him. If his master gave him a wife and she bore him sons or daughters, the woman and her children belong to the master . . . If a man buys a female slave to give to his son, he is to treat her like a daughter. If a man takes a second wife, he must continue to give his first wife the same amount of food and clothing and the same rights that she had before. If he does not fulfill these duties to her, he must set her free and not receive any payment.[2]

And again:

> If a fellow Israelite, man or woman, sells himself to you as a slave, you are to release him after he has served you for six years. When the seventh year comes, you must let him go free. When you set him free, do not send him away empty-handed. Give to him generously from what the Lord has blessed you with - sheep, grain, and wine. Remember that you were slaves in Egypt and the Lord your God set you free; that is why I am now giving you this command. . . . But your slave may not want to leave; he may love you and your family and be content to stay. Then take him to the door of your house and there pierce his

< 53 >

ear; he will then be your slave for life. Treat your
female slave in the same way. Do not be resentful
when you set a slave free; after all, he has served you
for six years at half the cost of a hired servant. Do
this, and the Lord your God will bless you in all that
you do.[3]

58. One only needs to compare these passages with the
celebrated quote from Aristotle: "If every tool could
perform its own work when ordered . . . like the statues
of Daedalus in the story or the tripods of Hephaestus
which the poet says 'enter self-moved the company of
the divine'—if thus shuttles wove and quills played
harps of themselves, mastercraftsmen would have no
need of assistants and masters no need of slaves."[4]
Historically at the same level of technological sophistication, and at the same level of social organization
(mainly around the household economy), the two neighboring civilizations were ruled by social philosophies so
different that they faced themselves as two worlds apart.

The Greeks centered the purpose of their lives on the
concept of "leisure" and on what they called the "good
life," which was also the measure of freedom. Their
notion of community, *oikos*, was above all a hierarchical
structure in which the dominant goal was the well-
being of that *zoon politikon* which is the citizen, the sole
household master and lord. For him alone the household
was to provide welfare, namely material goods, and
something more, the gift of *leisure*, free time for the
practice of *sophrosyne*—the splendid classical ideal of
wholeness, balance and temperance. By the time of
Epicurus, the aim of one's life was happiness in that very
non-economic sense which is freedom from pain and a
sort of sublime indifference to external labors and strug-

< 54 >

gles known as *ataraxia*. "Some friends drink or throw dice together, others practice gymnastics and hunt or philosophize together; each sort spending their time together in the activity they love best of everything else in life."[5]

Not so for the desert nations faced with constant risks and changing fortunes. Among these peoples, the Jewish nation strictly observed the rules of humility under the unpredictable will of gods. The Lord your God and the Desert Nature that he stands for require caution, strict discipline and management of resources. By obeying the commandments, a nation can "live a long time in the rich and fertile land" that is not like the rest of the surrounding desert land where one "has to work hard to plant the grain and irrigate the fields." For this people, trading the barren desert for the "mountains and valleys watered by rain" is what the good life and its rewards are all about.

> Obey the commands that I have given you today; love the Lord your God and serve him with all your heart. If you do, he will send rain on your land when it is needed, in the autumn and in the spring, so that there will be grain, wine, and olive oil for you and grass for your livestock. You will have all the food you want. Do not let yourselves be led away from the Lord to worship and serve other gods. If you do, the Lord will become angry with you. He will hold back the rain, and your ground will become dry for crops to grow. Then you will soon die there, even though it is a good land that he is giving you.[6]

59. For "remember that you were slaves in Egypt" and you can fall at any time, again, prey to other nations and to the fate of slavery, or you can endure the misfortunes brought by a changing nature that might bring back the

< 55 >

days of hunger and thirst. Remember that good luck is a whimsical god and there is no ever-lasting gift even in the bountiful land of promise. Other nations are eyeing your real estate and one's fortune is another one's prize. In the open desert, better beware. Keep strict observance of the rules and don't let your house be divided.

60. This central notion of the community as the survival unit is reinforced in every call for the rule of Law. The Kantian categorical imperative is the old covenant's supreme principle. Serve your God, which is to serve your community, for what is right for the community is a maxim for every member. A sui-generis *Critique of Practical Reason,* the *Septuagint* book of ethics is founded on the principles of secular religion.

61. This is quite different from the ideal of leisure as "the sister of freedom," (in Aelian's words[7]) which makes possible one's cultivation of excellence and is the condition of virtue and of belonging to the class of the *chosen.* To the Greco-Romans, moral consciousness, which among the Greeks is identical with the sense of *beautiful,* was possible only in the presence of a specific condition, that of servile labor. The aim of politics in the largest Aristotelian sense was to organize this two tier society: activity performed under servitude at the bottom, and the pursuit of happiness and excellence among friends and citizens at the top—the ultimate purpose of good household economy.

Class-based morality, in which social division rather than unity, i.e. one's salvation against another's servitude, is indeed the system of Greek city-state. The principle of the division of labor now comes to signify the divorce of moral consciousness from human consciousness. On the one hand—melancholy and idleness,

< 56 >

the poetry of self-idolatry and narcissism which is the gnomic lyric of a Solon or a Theognis who prefer death to life and esteem them happy who have never been born or who die young. On the other hand—coercion under direct compulsion or the dictates of sheer need, slavery for those self-moving machines engaged in the eternal filling of the Danaides' sieves or in fulfilling the eternal work of Sisyphus.

Individualism is the law of the Greek republic with the inevitable consequences of cynicism and alienation.

On the contrary, the national covenant is the law of the Jewish community, with the inevitable consequences of collective self-idolatrization and, throughout its history, intolerance to collective reinvention and evolution.

There were other ways too in which the ancient Middle East societies were able to combine state interests with self-styled class interests. One such model was the totalitarian structure of the Egyptian civilization, another model was the short-lived Assyrian militaristic organization that helped it rise to prominence. But they remained local systems with little direct continuing in the life of the world.

62. The Greco-Roman world and the Jewish community outlived their own time and have remained competitive and at odds with each other ever since. While both successful, they differ fundamentally. It happened that while the *internal* division within the Greek society set the chosen minority of free citizens against the wretched many, by the same token the *external* divorce of the Jewish community as a whole from social/historical progression sets it against the rest of the world.

< 57 >

National vs. Religious

63. One has only to remove himself from the notions of regional history and indulge in the indifference of the cosmopolitan world view in order to escape the trap of the traditional concepts that still haunt us. *Nation* and *religion* remain the two pillars of human collective identification.

In the age of nation-states, nationalism emerged as the all-consuming social passion. In other times, religion defines the line between good and evil. Combined, the national-religion results in unchecked fanaticism.

"How terrible for you, teachers of the Law and Pharisees! You hypocrites! You sail the seas and cross whole countries to win one convert; and when you succeed, you make him twice as deserving of going to hell as you yourself are!"[8] Is Jewishness a nation or a religion? Is Judaism the religion of the Jewish nation?

64. Ethnic and racial mix—whether Sephardi or Ashkenazi, Mediterranean, Indian or Ethiopian Jews—did Jewish peoples' religion outweigh their racial makeup?

65. By the time of the Babylonian captivity and then the return to Israel, the Pentateuch had been given definite form (after 538 B.C), although infused with heavy elements of earlier Babylonian mythology. The Assyro-Babylonian cult of Marduk (Merodach) and Ishtar (Esther), the account given by Enuma-Elish (the inspira-

< 58 >

tion for *Genesis*), and the narrative of Ut-Napishtim
from Gilgamesh (the source for the defluvium) were
spread under different names throughout the closely
interrelated world of the Middle East and were integrated into the core of the Jewish cultural heritage.

From the religious reform ordered by Josiah (621 BC)
that asserted strict central control over the institutions
of the cult, up to the drastic measures taken by Nehemiah (446 BC), with the assent of King Artaxerses, to
govern Judah and rebuild the temple of Jerusalem, when
Nehemiah "purified the [Jewish] people from everything
foreign,"[9] the universe of the Old Testament is imbued
with conquests, movements of people across the lands
between Nile and Euphrates, riches that were accumulated and lost, loves that consumed the spirit and the
flesh, jealousies that were avenged, intruders who came
from afar and arrivistes who moved up, kingdoms that
were achieved through acts of astute manipulation and
lost to new faster rivals, mass exodus out of yearning for
better prospects, battles waged for limited resources as
well as for the immense wealth of the day's most powerful men.

66. In Greece, by the same time, early 6th century BC,
Thales of Miletus was making the old Aryan myth of the
heavenly Okeanos into a scientific foundation for modern physics. The water of the storm-cloud, he told his
disciples, fructifies the earth and is the father of all
living things.[10] It was even said that he predicted the
eclipse of the 28th of May, 585 BC and that he was
acquainted with the phenomenon of magnetism, as well
with the attractive property of polished amber (apeiron).
But, more than any other Greek, Xenophanes (6th century BC) set the anti-mythology attitude of his nation's
coming of age. His impact on Greek society, one might

< 59 >

say, was not unlike that of the Hebrew prophets' impact on Jewish society as they stood vigilant against polytheism and idolatry. With eloquence and irony, he started out as the creator of the avant-garde *philosophical monotheism*. His satires, as we know them today mainly from Aristotle, combat the error of those who infinitely multiply the divine Being, who attribute to it a human form (anthropomorphism) and human passions (anthropopathism). *There is one God,* he says, *only one God, comparable to the gods of Homer or to mortals neither in form nor in thought.* Being immutable and immovable, it has no need of going about, now hither, now thither, in order to carry out its wishes, but without toil it governs all things by thought alone. Furthermore, from the point of view of ordinary mortals (Homer's and Hesiod's accepted authority) gods are imagined as being born as humans are, as having feelings and passions like a human's. They ascribe to their gods all things that are a shame and disgrace among men—theft, adultery, and, more important yet, falsehood. They do what the oxen or lions would, could they, Xenophanes says with philosophical sarcasm: they would represent them in the form of lions or oxen.

In place of these imaginary beings, let us adore the one infinite Being, who bears us in his bosom, and in whom there is neither generation nor corruption, neither change nor origin.[11]

67. The beginning of Greek philosophy and modern metaphysical thinking started with the words of this paradox: The first question of abstract reflection that arouses passions is the problem of *becoming*. *Being* persists, *beings* constantly change; they are born and they pass away. How could *Being* change and yet be eternal? How can *Being* both persist and perish? The

< 60 >

quest for an answer, both metaphysical and empirical, had just taken off.

In Greek society, the intellectual search for self-understanding was made possible by the existence of a masterful upper-class removed from the ordinary pursuit of survival. The idleness of the leisure class came to the rescue of the existential inquiry.

Undemocratic and not answerable to its mass constituency—its *internal proletariat*—Hellenistic high society was the first European group to acquire prominence and maintain its unchallenged paradigm of success against any *external elite*, and those were the older elites of the Middle Eastern civilizations, the Egyptian, the Assyrian, the Persian.

Of course, the heavy costs and the payloads incurred by the international triumph were thrust on the plebeians and the lower-class, the unsophisticated, ill-bred and ill-mannered, the base, earthy, commoners, cheap lives and inferior, the mere talking implements, unworthy of human life, ruled by low desires, instincts and animal impulses, prey to misrepresentation, delusion and falsehood, incongruous and inconsistent, corrupt and wicked, consumed by immorality, fetishism and promiscuity—outcasts relegated to the low end of the social division of labor.

The social compact itself was remodeled thus by a warrior mentality into an adversarial relationship. With that we enter the European modern age.

< 61 >

Social vs. National

68. One might draw a parallel between European class-based societies and the long-lasting Eastern slave-based civilizations, from the Indian caste-society to the Oriental despot-states throughout the ancient world. Yet they differ fundamentally in that the character of the class conflict in the European societies was dynamic, as opposed to the static social division in the Oriental societies.

The dissimilarity between the two models of socially divided worlds is revealed best by the institutionalization of class warfare in the Hellenic city-states. Thucydides, the historian, describes it in its earliest phases, as it manifested in the state of Corcyra: "Such was the savagery of the class-war at Corcyra as it developed, and it made the deeper impression through being the first of its kind—though eventually the upheaval spread through almost the whole Hellenic World . . . So the countries of Hellas became infected with class-war, and the sensation made by each successive outbreak had a cumulative effect upon the next."[12] And, one can add, it certainly still has.

69. Oriental monarchies, while highly polarized socially, were also hierarchically and organically integrated top-down; a tightly-controlled bureaucratic, monolithic social structure. Equally subjected to the despot-dictator, all members of the society were linked together by the chain of command down to their lowest destinies.

< 62 >

By contrast, in the European state, individualism remains the over arching principle.

The Hellenic society grew up upon an elite warrior mentality: the subjugation and the exploitation of its occupied inhabitants, in contrast to the millenary-old covenant-bound Jewish nation, a refined symbiosis of heterogeneous constituencies. Two worlds apart.

70. One practiced a highly motivated, high achieving drive to subdue new frontiers; the other was committed to a managerial life style. One stood for competitive accomplishment; the other sought social harmony and integration. One plunged into the abyss of philosophical knowledge and aspiration for external beauty, the Ideal; the other focused its energies on mastering the esoterics of the social contract. One took on political leadership within the Mediterranean basin; the other avoided head-on conflict with the outside world and chose rather to seek its weak spots. One conquered by sword; the other followed the Laws. One subdued every corner of the Old World; the other settled in every quarter.

While the Greeks opened the Pandora's box of activism, knowledge, and industry, the Jews were capitalizing on their long trek through the history of the Middle East.

As the New World moved westward, the Old World of the Middle East civilizations collapsed. Their cultural relics, reduced to mere symbols, were made into a guide book to help the scattered remnants of tribes preserve their civilization.

By the time those works were given definite form—after 538 BC—the days of Middle Eastern people's influence

< 63 >

on world affairs, as gate keepers of the Eastern Trade Centers, were gone, since business was reduced to a trickle. Times had changed.

Faced with these changes, and under repeated blows from the Greco-Roman new world order, the old nation split: some continued the old ways and copied over and over the ancestral scrolls; some set about revisiting and updating the core tenets. Revolution from within was the biggest single event in what was by now the atavistic heir of the Middle Eastern cultural paradigm, and it was administered by a man named Joshua—whom some called Christ, in the hope that the long awaited rejuvenator had come, the Messiah.

71. The old myth of the uniqueness of Jewish monotheistic thinking has its appeal but little validity.

Indeed, various intellectual ideas often develop concurrently; but they are not recognized as being the same. They differ not only in their adherents' strictly observed jargon but also in their cultural ontogeny. So that, while the Hellenistic consciousness divided itself into a monotheistic philosophical mind and a polytheistic folk mythology, the Jewish consciousness split itself off from the diverse cultural conglomerates, and affirmed itself as a monotheistic community.

The average Greek folk, in the highly inequitable class-divided Western-style society, were probably inferior in skills and wisdom to the average member of the more homogeneous Jewish community. But while the latter system produced good average citizens, that was outweighed by the outstanding individual achievements recorded throughout the Greco-Roman world. The Jewish system offered protection and appurtenance to a

< 64 >

strong team, but it took away the sense of brevity and
'the Promethean vein of the individual's scorn for as-
cribed destiny. It also removed the flash of temperament
and heroic tragedy that produce the lone maverick and
the philosopher-king.

The Greeks lived independently, owed nothing to their
community scattered among abundant natural resources, daring to confront and defy each other; unruly,
distrustful, analytical, and individualistic. They prized
astute action and believed in pragmatic knowledge. They
awarded their champions with the misery of the losers. -
They produced Apollonian geniuses on the heights of the
Acropolis and a valley of mud that surrounded its white
colonnades.

Two political paradigms, the class system versus the
communitarian system, set off on their journey for the
end of history. The Middle Eastern communitarian system was derived from the demands imposed by dependency on vast irrigation works, at its turn dependent on
access to a limited supply of fertile riverine lands. At
first, the West was awed by the success of such a system;
then the Sophist squared off with the bizarre and the
impenetrable Talmudist. And everything changed.

72. At the dawning of the first millennium A D, a
strange development was taking place in the social
consciousness of the Roman Empire. A curious mania
had appeared, as Seneca observed—a peculiar taste for
death, a facile propensity for suicide overtook not only
the courageous, but sometimes the cowardly as well;
some killed themselves out of loathing for their lives,
some out of spleen and boredom. Many could not bear to
see and do endlessly the same thing. Not that they
detested their lives in any material sense, but they were

< 65 >

repulsed by life's prosaic drag along a hopeless treadmill of all-the-same routines, and they were tormented by the perennial question: what will the end be like? You woke up, slept, woke up again, felt the cold, the heat, the cold—always the same thing. Night followed day, summer followed spring, then fall, winter, spring again, the same thing passed away only to return again, one generation goes, another will follow it just the same, soon: This was unbearable; people quit life not because it was harsh but because it was futile, remarked Seneca.[13]

Here, for the first time, the spontaneous natural philosophy that had started with the Greeks centuries earlier, and which the Western spirit professed to emulate, turned on its head.

73. Western philosophy's monistic premises were set up back in the times of Parmenides and his mentor, Xenophanes. Since there is no change in God, according to Xenophanes, God is everything. Hence, what we call change, said Parmenides, is but an appearance, an illusion, and there is in reality neither origin nor decay; ergo, the eternal being alone exists.

This metaphysical truth failed, at the time, to stir the passions of the general masses. However, the thesis was of sufficient interest to become the subject of a philosophical poem authored by Xenophanes, preserved to this day as the most ancient instance in our possession of metaphysical speculation among the Greeks.[14] It was also the source of all kinds of trouble for the late Western sophist. Ironically, the poet started with the question of Truth. With youthful and enthusiastic passion, he demonstrates by means of specious argument that our notions of change, plurality, and limitation contradict reason. It all seemed so straightforward.

< 66 >

Starting with the idea of *being*, he seemed to have proven that that which *is* cannot *have become* what it is, nor could it cease to be, nor become something else; for if *being* began to exist, it was either its own product or it came from non-being. Now, in the former case, if it is its own product, it has created itself, which is to say that it did not originate—that it is eternal. The latter case supposes that something can come from nothing, which is absurd. For the same reasons, that which exists can neither change nor perish, for in death it would pass into either being or non-being. If being is changed into being, then it does not change; and to assert that it becomes nothing is as illogical as to say that it comes from nothing. Consequently, being is eternal, et cetera, et cetera.

The trouble is that the universe, which reason conceives as an indivisible unity, is divided by the senses. Hence our knowledge of the perceived universe is pervaded by illusion, as Parmenides sadly acknowledges. The possibility of knowledge is undermined by the uncertainty of our means.

Parmenides already called our attention to the many illusions in which the senses involve us. Next, Zeno, the Stoic, also questioned the truth but still allowed for it as a possibility. Then, Socrates went one step further: 'One thing alone I know, and that is that I know nothing'—which is ambiguous, but optimistic nevertheless. Arcesilaus exaggerated his skepticism and declared: 'I do not even know that, with certainty.' Still, the optimistic attitude prevailed in a general sense throughout most of the Greek classical age.

Aristotle decided to ignore the sophistic argumentation

< 67 >

on the metaphysics of Truth and remained a zealot scientist and a dogmatic believer in freethinking. Following him, the Stoics also relied on science in the search for Providence in nature and in history. And so did the Epicureans, for whom science alone could free man from superstition and prejudice, and make happiness possible. Both schools agreed that there was a criterion for truth.

Enter the Skeptics. No two schools of philosophy agree on the essential problems, said Pyrrho of Elis, a contemporary of Aristotle and a friend of Alexander the Great. Hence, instead of procuring peace, knowledge involves us in endless contradictions, disputes without end, since one can in every case prove both the affirmative and the negative side. The essence of things is incomprehensible.

But most of all Carneades, with dialectical skill, brought out the contradictions involved in the monistic belief in truth: If God exists, he is either a finite or an infinite being. If he is finite, he forms a *part* of the whole of things, he is part of All and not the complete, total, and perfect Being. If he is infinite, he is immutable, immovable, and without modification or sensation; which means that he is not a living and real being. Hence, God cannot be conceived as either a finite or an infinite being. If he exists, he is either incorporeal or corporeal. If he has no body, he is insensible; if he has a body, he is not eternal. God is virtuous or without virtue; and what is a virtuous God but a God who recognizes the good as a law that is superior to his will, i.e., a god who is not the Supreme Being? On the other hand, would not a god without virtue be inferior to a virtuous man? The notion of God is therefore a contradictory one, however one may conceive its attributes.

< 68 >

From here to that curious mania that Seneca describes is only a short ride. The superior class of intellectual who so assertively started its quest for "the Good" and "the Truth" lost its way. The wise men of the West lost their minds. The professors went mad!

They left the simple folk of the Greco-Roman colonies with no spiritual leaders; without a queen, the worker bees saw their queen fly away—and they went berserk.

74. One consequence of such a philosophical vacuum is rendered in the tragic character of popular justice that ravaged Rome with soulless violence for a hundred years from Sulla to Octavianus. The mob of Rome punished criminals not out of justice, love of truth, or moral values, which they were supposedly defending, but out of its own free will. The mob, this monster with one hundred heads, said Tacitus, was more powerful than the free will of the individuals, and thus, they were unlawfully killing the unlawful and any punishment of guilt was a new guilt in itself the more horrifying as it was not a curse on one single individual but on the whole nation.

The moral quest, the intellectual conflict between what is just and unjust, between right and wrong, between means and ends, between one and many, for the first time in modern history surpassed the bounds of the academic or temple community. It spilled over into the streets and the arenas of the mob's fervor.

The philosophical-religious questions of what life is all about, and whether life itself make sense at all, the purpose of life's laborious, demanding, troublesome course were no longer played out only in the *agora* of academia. The debate devolved into a physical conflict.

< 69 >

The tragic street battle pitted men against men, yet the conflict that erupted involved higher level actors—it was the clash between the universal character of the state, and the individuals that comprised it.

75. If the metaphysical God proved unsustainable, so was the religious God. It was Christ that applied the last blow to the God in heaven.

> Then some Pharisees and teachers of the Law came from Jerusalem to Jesus and asked him, 'Why is it that your disciples disobey the teaching handed down by our ancestors? They don't wash their hands in the proper way before they eat!'
>
> Jesus answered, 'And why do you disobey God's command and follow your own teaching? For God said, "Respect your father and your mother", and "Whoever curses his father or his mother is to be put to death." But you teach that if a person has something he could use to help his father and his mother, but says, "This belongs to God," he does not need to honor his father. In this way you disregard God's command, in order to follow your own teaching. You hypocrites! How right Isaiah was when he prophesied about you!
>
> 'These people,' says God, 'honor me with their words, but their heart is really far away from me. It is no use for them to worship me, because they teach man-made rules as though they were my laws!'[15]

God in heaven, says Jesus, is man-made and therefore is not to be worshiped. Man-made rules, rites, liturgies and sacred services are not part of the commandments and are not godly. Godness is godlessness because it is humanism. Godness is social humanism and morality. Godness is anti-'God.'

< 70 >

> As Jesus was starting on his way again, a man ran up,
> knelt before him, and asked him, "Good Teacher,
> what must I do to receive eternal life?" "Why do you
> call me good?" Jesus asked him. "No one is good
> except God alone. You know the commandments: Do
> not commit adultery; do not steal; do not accuse
> anyone falsely; do not cheat; respect your father and
> your mother."

The book of rational ethics is Christ's exhortation. While
he seemingly speaks in terms of religious orthodoxy and
teaches a return to the fundamental tenets and commandments of the Hebrew God, we may readily perceive
his practical rationalism. He proclaims atheism and
moral philosophy in the name of theism; in the name of
the Divine, he affirms human reason and the means of
rational knowledge. "Why are you discussing about not
having bread? Don't you know or understand yet? Are
your minds so dull?" He is so far detached from asserting
the idea of God's transcendence, or human dependency
on transcendental manifestations of the divine, that
whatever might be in heaven, he states, is decided here.
"And so I tell all of you: what you prohibit on earth will
be prohibited in heaven, and what you permit on earth
will be permitted in heaven."[16]

By virtue of the existing universal harmony, of the
rational manifestation of the universe, there must be
agreement between divine reason (whatever that might
be) and human reason; a radical opposition between the
human mind and the universal law is not conceivable.
Owing to this agreement, man *naturally* possesses godly
powers and lives by the universal rules of goodness and
of justice.

> Who, then, can be saved?" he is asked, and the answer is
> blunt: "Jesus looked straight at them and answered: 'This

< 71 >

is impossible for man."[17] All one can look for is to live virtuously: "Anyone who leaves home or brothers or sisters or mother or father or children or fields for me and for the gospel, will receive much more in this present age. He will receive a hundred times more houses, brothers, sisters, mothers, children, and fields—and persecutions as well."[18]

Two great questions dominate the teaching of the new gospel. One is the relationship between the individual and God—between human liberty and divine omnipotence. The other is the relationship between man and mankind—between the individual and the state. The answer to the first question was within oneself. The answer to the second was within the first answer.

What is Godly is what is 'humanly'!

76. The paradox of the Trinity is what troubled most the later Christians for at the very heart of it lay a dogma that the Christians themselves proclaimed to be absurd. Against the vehement objections of an articulate minority—the Arians—the Council of Nicea (325) had laid down that Jesus, the son of god, was consubstantial with his father, and thus, an equal partner in the Trinity which included as its third component the Holy Spirit. That was a theological subterfuge to hide the contradictions of the dogma itself. For until then, it was not the theologians who were the real patrons of the new teachings, but the aspiration of the populace at large for an acknowledgment of their legitimacy as human individuals. And their god, Christ himself, was a man.

The message was of freedom, and that was understood only by those who were deprived of freedom.

< 72 >

No gods, no soothsaying and superstition, no mystery, fear, punishment, submission to priests and civil servants, no more apprehension, reverence to sophists and abstruse academics, no obedience and compliance to their masters—freedom was within oneself! A true Copernican revolution was possible, and it meant an about-face from outer authority to individual liberty. It meant redeemed dignity and self-respect.

Throughout the Roman world, the system of slavery had debased the slave-descended urban proletarian and deprived him of his sense of self-worth. In the words of historian A. J. Toynbee: "A long-drawn-out life-in-death was the penalty of failure to respond to the challenge of enslavement, and no doubt that broad path of destruction was trodden by the majority of those human beings of many different .origins and antecedents who were enslaved *en masse* in the most evil age of Hellenic history."[19] And now, the same terrifying Roman authorities were seeing the miracle of a faith in liberty, "performed quite under their eyes and repeated—in defiance of their efforts to arrest it by physical force."

People called their new conviction the religion of Christ, when in reality was the doctrine of liberation from religion and the proclamation of a man, Christ, as the new Spartacus, this time an invincible leader because he was within every one of his army of countless individual souls and bodies. His own revolution was now a myriad of revolutions, a tidal wave, an endless upsurge of insurgents.

By no coincidence, as early as the year 211, virtually all inhabitants of the Roman empire were granted Roman citizenship by Caracalla. Only four hundred years later, under Justinian, the distinction between "ingenui"

< 73 >

(slaves by birth) and "liberti" was abolished for good. This event marked at once, the eradication of the institution of slavery as such in the Western European world and gave lifeblood to the doctrine of liberation theology.

An individualistic revolutionary, an insubordinate, a mutinous, rebellious man became the role model, the symbol, the inspiration for generations to come. The message was no longer one of appeasing the existing order, was no longer one of submission to the tribe's or the establishment's oppressive demands. It blared forth the example of individualistic dissidence and defiance, approval for the pursuit of one's own dignity and self-worth.

In Christ, generations to come found legitimacy for their own ego and insubordination. Christ became the symbol of the anti-authority sentiment, of the godly irreligious insurrection.

< 74 >

3
Dialectical History

77. We have looked, in previous chapters, at the Western mind as the product of the convergence between the individualistic Greco-Roman world and the community-centered Middle-Eastern-Jewish consciousness. This product is still developing continuously on the wave of what Giambattista Vico calls "corsi i recorsi." Swinging between the individual-liberating democratic tendencies and individual-restricting calls for the rule of order, Western life-cycles of historical development, while preserving the unity of a community, have generated throughout modern history enough inconsistency and dissention from within to have ignited the engines of what can be called *sectarian individualism.*

Says Vico: "Governments, early on, were unitary: the domestic monarchies were great patriarchal families; then, simultaneously with the rise of the aristocracy of

< 77 >

the heroic ages, they passed into the hands of a larger
but still restricted number of individuals; later on, they
extended to the many and they have ended by belonging
to everybody in the popular republics where all citizens
(or a majority) contribute to the political chores and the
political leadership; finally, in civil monarchies, they
have returned to unitary government. The nature of
numbers offers a division or succession not unlike that
suggested by the concept of unity, the restricted number,
the large number and the whole, such that each term of
the succession—namely few, many and all—preserve,
each one in its own nature, the principle of unity."[1]

Subsequently, Hegel enlarged the concept of history,
giving it a dialectical dimension. The concept of history
was now derived from the immanent principle of nature
as the rational spirit in a process of self generation, a
generator of the absolute itself. What was Absolute was
the process, which is to say the immanent reason within
nature.

The contradiction found in the idea of being was to be
resolved in the notion of becoming. Being becomes, i.e.,
determines itself, limits itself, defines itself. But determi-
nate, or *finite*, being continues *ad infinitum*; the finite is
infinite. The contradiction is resolved, in Hegel's terms,
in the notion of *individuality*, which is the unity of the
two. To consider otherwise would be to hold the two
sides as mutually exclusive, which means that the infinite would be limited by the finite, or would be finite
itself. If the infinite begins where the finite ends, and if
the finite begins where the infinite ends, so that the
infinite is *beyond* the finite, it would not really be
infinite. The infinite is the essence of the finite, and the
finite is the manifestation of the infinite, of infinite
existence. Infinity determines itself, limits itself, sets

< 78 >

boundaries to itself; in a word, it becomes the finite by the very fact that it gives itself existence. Existence is possible only under certain conditions, in certain modes, or within certain limits. Existence is self-limitation. Existence is finite being.[2]

78. As in nature so in society: The blind forces manifested in the state of nature, e.g., the instinct for the propagation of the species and the instinct for reprisal of wrong and harmful continue but change their form. They become marriage and legal punishment: regulated, disciplined instincts, ennobled by the law.

In Hegelian idiom, the objective mind, i.e., objective order, manifests itself in the form of *right*, which is freedom conceded and guaranteed to all. The individual who is recognized as free is a *person*. The personality realizes and asserts itself through *property*. Each legal person has, by virtue of his free activity, the right to possess, and consequently, also the right to transfer his property. This transference takes place in the form of a *contract*. The contract is the *State* in embryo.

Right, i.e. Law, appears in the fullness of its power only when individual caprice opposes the general will (the objective mind, which is objective order). The conflict between the individual will and the general will is parallel to the convergence of the civil society into the State.

79. Civil society, grounded in the family, is not yet the State. Its aim is still only the protection of individual interests. Hence civil society is an intermediate stage which prevails in smaller countries, Hegel continues, where society and the State are identical. Civil society as such disappears with the formation of great united

< 79 >

states. There, the State differs from civil society in that it no longer solely pursues the good of individuals, but aims at the realization of an *idea*, for which it does not hesitate to sacrifice private interests. The State is the kingdom of the idea, of the universal, of the *objective* goal ("mind"), for the fulfillment of which the family and civil society are merely means.

The *republic* is not, according to Hegel, the most perfect form of government. Ultimately resting upon the confusion of civil society with the State, it exaggerates the importance and the role of the individual. The republics of antiquity were superseded by dictatorships because they sacrificed the *idea* to the individual, the family, and the caste. In the Greek Tyranny and Roman Caesarism, sovereign reason itself condemns the radical vice of the republican, democratic, and aristocratic forms of government.

In Hegel's view, monarchy is the normal political form. In the free and sovereign action of a unipersonal ruler, the national idea finds adequate expression. The State is nothing but an abstraction unless personified in a monarch—the depositary of its power, its political traditions, and the idea which it is called upon to realize. The prince is the State made man, impersonal reason become conscious reason, the general will become personal will. That is, according to our philosopher, the true meaning of Louis XIV's epigraph: *l'Etat c'est moi.*

It is worth refreshing our reading of Hegel by pointing to one more component of his thinking. Despite appearances to the contrary, Hegel argues, the most vigorous people in the State, representing the most viable idea, always succeed in gaining mastery. History is merely an incessant struggle between States of the past and those

< 80 >

of the future. The idea of the State is gradually realized by means of such defeats and victories. The historical States are the temporary forms in which they appear, discarded when time has worn them out, only to assume new forms. Since the absolute is not restricted to a particular existence, but always found in the whole, we cannot say that the ideal State is anywhere. The ideal State is everywhere and nowhere: everywhere, because it tends to realize itself in historical States; nowhere, for as an ideal, it is a problem to be solved by the future. History is the progressive solution of the political problem. Every nation adds its stone to the building of the ideal State, but each people also carries on its "original sin" (its finite existence), which is brought into opposition with the idea and thus, sooner or later, it encompasses its own ruin. Each State represents the ideal from a certain side; none realizes it in its fullness; none, therefore, is immortal.

Each nation in turn succumbs to another and transmits to its successors, in a more developed and enlarged form, the political idea of which it has been the depositary, the civilization of which it has been the guardian.

The passing of civilization from one people to another constitutes the *dialectics of history*, an expression which is not taken figuratively by Hegel. Reason is the innermost substance of history, which is logic in action. In the eyes of the superficial historian, empires rise, flourish, and decline, peoples struggle, and armies destroy each other. But behind these nations and their armies are the principles they represent; behind the ramparts and the batteries, ideas battle each other.

In the development of the States of Greece, the earlier sluggishness of Asia Minor is followed by political life

< 81 >

and its fruitful conflicts; they concluded first into the absolute monarchy, which again was superseded by the republic. Here as a happy form of civil society, individuals are no longer modes with which the *substance* of the State has nothing to do, but integral parts of a whole, which exists only through them; as such they have a sense of their importance, and appreciate that the State needs their cooperation. The classical republic lasts as long as the individual elements and the State remain in equilibrium. They are imperiled as soon as the demagogue's *regime* substitutes for the national interest the selfish interests of individual ambition. The Caesarian reaction forces the rebellious individual into obedience; the habitable world is conquered; the most diverse nations are thrown into one and the same mould and reduced to an inert and powerless mass.

80. The three phases of every evolution—being, expansion and concentration—recur in the three great cycles of history. "The ancient division of constitutions into monarchy, aristocracy, and democracy is based upon the notion of substantial, still undivided unity, a unity which has not yet come to its inner differentiation (to a matured, internal organization) and which therefore has not yet attained depth or concrete rationality. From the standpoint of the ancient world, therefore, this division is the true and the correct one, since for a unity of that still substantial type, a unity inwardly too immature to have attained its absolutely complete development, difference is essentially an external difference and appears at first as a difference in the number of those in whom that substantial unity is supposed to be immanent . . . Consequently, it is quite idle to inquire which of the three is most to be preferred. *Such forms must be discussed historically or not at all.*[3]

< 80 >

Scholastic Theology, the State and the Republic

81. The equilibrium between the State and the individual is restored in the Christian universalist political body as a sui-generis new type of world monarchy.

Whether in theological terms or on the battlefields of the medieval Europe, the only affliction, benign but chronic nevertheless, that strained the otherwise logical construct of celestial as well as terrestrial Christendom was the not so nonsensical controversy between the *realists* and the *nominalists*—for this centuries-long "monkish quarrel"[4] of the Scholastics was in reality a metaphysical conflict that only amplified the more substantial medieval political imbalances.

The Catholic or *universal* Church does not merely aim to be an aggregation of particular Christian communities and of the believers composing them; it regards itself as a superior power, as a reality distinct from and independent of the individuals belonging to the fold. If the idea, that is, the general or universal, were not a *reality*, the "Church" would be a mere collective term, and the particular churches, or rather the individuals composing them, would be the only *realities*. Hence, the Church must be realistic[5] and declare with the Academy: *universalia sunt realia*. Catholicism is synonymous with realism.

Commonsense, on the other hand, tends to regard universals as mere notions of the mind, as signs designating a collection of individuals, as abstractions having no

< 83 >

objective reality. According to this, individuals alone are real, and the dictum used by the nominalists was: *Universalia sunt nomina.*

William of Champeaux brought the consequences of *realism* to its extreme conclusion. According to him, nothing is real but the universal; individuals are mere *flatus vocis.* From the anthropological point of view, for example, there is in reality, according to Champeaux, but *one* man, the universal man, the man-type, the genus man. All individuals are fundamentally the same and differ only in the accidental modifications of their common essence.

The nominalist view, advanced by Roscellinus, seemed quite harmless at first, as the full magnitude of its heresy was concealed from the eyes of the Church. Yet the implications of such unorthodox reasoning were not favorable to the institution of the Church and its hierarchy. If the individual alone is real, it follows that the Church itself is but a *flatus vocis;* the individuals composing it are the only realities. If the individual alone is real, Catholicism is no more than a collection of individual convictions and there is nothing real, solid, and positive but the personal faith of the Christian. Again, if the individual alone is real, there is nothing real in God either, except the three persons: the Father, the Son, and the Holy Ghost, while the common essence which, according to the Church, unites them into one God, is mere *nomen,* a spoken syllable.

In uncertain terms, here is the same old antinomy of all times, our times included.

82. The same ambiguity holds true for concepts such as idealism/materialism, subjective/objective, individual/

< 84 >

state, and so on:

That same ambiguity afflicts even that cornerstone of nineteenth century materialism, i.e., the doctrine of the dialectical materialism, whose central concept, matter, is fatally flawed by definition. *Matter* is understood to be in opposition to the notion of either a subjective or an objective spirit, i.e. God, or idea; it is a philosophical category that designates the objective reality given to man through his sensations and perceptions, copied, photographed, mirrored by our senses and *existing independently of them* (Lenin).[6] The key point in this definition is that matter exists independently of our consciousness, or any abstract form of consciousness, whether the Hegelian Absolute Spirit or the subjective Holy spirit of Hume.

The materialist view is generally understood to stand for commonsense and empirical/intuitive science. However, trying to express it formally as a rational philosophical *principle of existence*, we run into one problem after another.

In removing any sort of physical, humanly perceptible particular substratum, form, or corporeal known state or substantial things, by reducing the essence of what is material to something above and beyond the manifest and perceptible substance, the inevitable consequence is the substitution of one abstraction with another abstraction. *For, ironically, the above definition of matter is a perfect and legitimate definition of God, absolute spirit, transcendental reason, universal mind, etc., under any hypostasis of the idealist principles of philosophy.* It reduces the entire issue of universal principles to a partisan view of the relationships between such abstract notions as *objective* reality and the *subjective* perception

< 85 >

thereof.

Thus, the dilemma: a consistently *materialistically* defined existence, as something outside of consciousness, makes room for the old specter of dualism; a tolerant materialism, by substituting existence as a whole, reason and consciousness included, for the notion of abstract matter, raises doubts about its own consistency. For God, too, is *matter.* God is nothing else but the philosophical category that denotes *objective* reality outside of and independent to our senses, revealed to man as nature through his senses.

Given this interchangeability of the abstract notions of God and matter, we have the odd reversal of terminology from the time of the Scholastics to the present day. The Scholastics used the term *realism* for what we now call *idealism.* What we call today *objective*, Scholastic philosophy called *subjective* (namely, that which exists as a transcendental subject—substance or reality independent of my thought); while what we call *subjective* was called *objective* (namely, that which exists merely as an *object* of thought and not as a real subject). This converse terminology is still found in Descartes and Spinoza.

For a Scholastic philosopher, our locution might appear as a strange confusion of ideas and issues. Intellectual chaos for one is rational order for another. *Consistent idealism* is *consistent materialism* turned inside out.

83. It took the barbarians of ancient Europe about a thousand years of cognitive effort to grasp antiquity's lost civilization which, in its death throws, handed over to them its own spiritual inheritance and emblem, which is Christianity. By the turn of the first millen-

< 86 >

nium, the newer heathens, the Visigoths, Ostrogoths, Lombards, Normans, Saxons as well as the Vandals, Huns, and the Slavs, even Turkomans, were already winding down their wild roaming and their frantic plundering in exchange for a few luxuries and a *mondaine* life. Cities accumulated riches, country manors propagated advanced agricultural techniques, populations expanded, covering the last patches of virgin land and steadily rediscovering the Middle East's lost experience. Trade, industry, travel, and money-based exchange of commodities brought unprecedented new manners and sophistication to the tribes living in the lands of forests and marshes.

Illustrative arts, in the beginning, then poetry, and Scholastic philosophy would usher the new leisure class of Renaissance prosperity into adventures of mind and pleasures of heart unbeknown or forbidden to their earlier crusader mentality. Between crude escapades, their untrained logical thinking gradually began to turn to questions that had exhausted their predecessors of the Greco-Roman empire: What is beyond our visible world? How can we achieve proven knowledge? Why is the world this way and where is the beginning? Reading lost books from legendary times seemed to offer a treasure of wisdom, and tinkering with mechanical constructs became a useful passion.

Overcoming a few natural disasters and local noblemen's wars, softening their ways and indulging in armchair chivalry rather than horseback crusades, the white men's tribal world slowly but inexorably turned into civic societies ruled by embryonic covenants, even experimenting with different political systems and forms of government. And, naturally, they produced their own political Plato and Aristotle in the writings of

< 87 >

Giambattista Vico and Niccolò Machiavelli.

84. When Roger Bacon looked around and asked: "Are we still just the same pygmies sitting on the shoulders of our cultural ancestors or are we, by now, giants on our own?"—it was time for Western European self-awareness to be born.

85. In France, Rousseau argued in favor of the General Will as a virtual "will in the best interest" of all, which is to say, the social will expressed not by the arithmetic tabulation of the popular vote—the majority of wills—but by the will of The Will. In this sense, for Rousseau and his closest interpreter, Bosanquet, the expression of social will rested with the social persona (the king, the ruling elite) and was not a result of social interactions among individuals. Communitarian philosophy was therefore founded on the will of the community bestowed upon the personified representative thereof: the enlightened king and his enlightened court. The chosen few were expected to act as a Hegelian impersonation of the Social Will, whether it be through Plato's Philosopher King, the Chief Priest, or the Secretary General. Ironically, that also equals the "general" will with a "particular" interest.

86. Such a view was in contrast to liberal democracy, which relied on existing individuals, real multitudes of wills, often at cross-purposes to each other. For John Locke or John Stuart Mill, the reality of the "wills of all" was the only source of social legitimacy and power. Their clashes of interests made up the substance of social life, and enshrined their constitutional sovereignty, whatever that may lead to, calamity or greatness. Whether the majority is right or not, is not the question; "right" is not the enlightened elite's monopoly either. For Locke *et al*, there is no capital-T Truth in the matter of General Good. The minority is not

< 88 >

fundamentally wrong per se, but is just one of the many sides of the loyal opposition. In a Rousseau-nian sense, democracy is truly synonymous with revolutionary acts of change from one governing elite to a new governing elite. Democracy is not the rule of the day but the exceptional break in the governing order. Not so in the populism of Americans James Madison and Thomas Jefferson, for whom the Enlightened establishment is a form of governing for undemocratic purposes, while the true and only democracy is possible in the daily pursuit and pragmatic exercise of the trades and the industry by the people for the people.

87. From here on it was conspicuously clear that European man had turned the tables. Learning from other nations, Western man proclaimed science and industry the new Law and the Commandments, and embarked on his own exodus out of the kingdom of idols. John Locke smashed the golden calf of prejudices and wrote on the scientific *tabula rasa* the new *experiential* matrix.

New developments made old ways obsolete. The Hesiodic epic of resignation, "days and work," became a celebration of Faustian industriousness. In its Hegeliano-German glorification, *becoming* was found to be eternal not only in a philosophical sense but in a material sense, as productive processes were forging raw materials into finished output throughout the steaming workshops and the smokestack mills of the land. Thus, the story itself of how things happened, the story of human destiny, was seen as multifarious and rather inconsistent reshaping and reinvention . . . contrary to the hitherto fundamental belief that there was constancy in this world.

88. From story, historiography became science. It sought causes and forces in history, as exemplified by Hegel.

< 89 >

Contingent became *necessity* and the message of history was revealed as a *living* totality in which cause was immanent in effect as the soul is in the body.

89. In the Prussian-Christian state of the early eighteenth century, Karl Marx could still horrify the establishment by speaking of "eating and clothing" as the primordial interests and forces of history: social life as being about real individuals, people of "flesh and blood," people as they are. Men are what they really are, Marx expounded. *Idealism* stood for the false idols that real men have in their closed minds.

A philosophy of man that is not based on the positive science of real individuals is hollow, Marx asserted in what came across as a courageous position. For that reason, once and for all, Marx called for a "ruthless criticism of everything existing;"—"Ruthless in two senses: The criticism must not be afraid of its own conclusions, nor of conflict with the powers that be."[7]

Marx's instigative lines are in no way unreasonable nowadays. Most educated people seem to agree with the statement that: "Consciousness can never be anything else than conscious existence, and the existence of men is their actual life-process." However, Marx went one step further, excluding that middle road hedging of the puzzle of history: "Ethics, religion, metaphysics and all other ideological domains, as well as their corresponding forms of consciousness, lose their appearance of independence. They have no history for themselves, they do not develop; but men, developing their material production and their material relationships, alter at once with this reality their thinking and the production of their thinking as well. Consciousness does not determine life, but life-process determines consciousness."[8]

< 90 >

Where does consciousness start? One might answer that it starts right where the life-process, existence, ends. Or does it? The muse only casts her eyes open wide at the *Riddle of History.*

90. Two great recurring aspirations have haunted modern European history, never to be achieved, although repeatedly sought by statesmen, philosophers, and large sections of the public: One was the yearning to recoup the lost *pan-European unity,* through the reenactment of the Holy Roman Empire, a political reality for a thousand years down to the fifth century and a myth for another millennium, to 1806. The second was the longing for the antedated mythical *Golden Age,* the lost paradise of community-based society.

The idea of the United European States was a high-level political vision. European unity was also sought under the name of all-worker's socialism.

Actually, the opposite was taking shape at a deeper and deeper level. And it was that very disintegration, conflict, dissent, the divisive clash of interests and the high concentration of competing civil entities, that was a curse and a blessing upon the European human race.

91. Like liberal capitalism's idealists, socialist philosophers like to refer to "real individuals, the living human individuals, people as they are." From that assertion, however, socialist leaders infer the moral imperative that sets the good of the general interest counter to individualistic self-interest and that principle then becomes a political imperative.

In a twist of history two social principles, individualism

< 91 >

versus the collective socialist movement turned the external conflict between the Hellenic-Roman world and the Middle Eastern social philosophy of classical antiquity into a conflict within the Western world itself.

< 92 >

4
Duns Scotus and the Industrial Revolution

92. Water is the first principle, according to Thales of Miletus, the universal substratum, of which the other bodies are mere modifications; water envelops the Earth on all sides; the Earth floats upon this infinite ocean, and constantly derives from it the nourishment it needs.

Philosophical principles notwithstanding, Thales correctly grasped water's life-giving qualities. Quintessential medium for trade and commerce, it was later said that water made economic life possible. It was the source of fertile soil along the valleys of the Nile, the Tigris and the Euphrates (not to mention the Ganges and the Yangtze). It allowed for low shipping costs across the Mediterranean basin, making it less expensive to ferry a cart load of wheat across the sea than to haul it twenty miles from the port of Ostia to Rome.

Creating and maintaining an international system of sea trade was the great achievement and one of the sustain-

< 95 >

ing pillars of the Greco-Roman civilization. To Adam Smith, writing about the wealth of maritime England, the importance of navigation in the life of nations was obvious. "The nations that, according to the best authenticated history, appear to have been first civilized, were those that dwelt round the coast of the Mediterranean Sea. That sea, by far the greatest inlet that is known in the world, having no tides, nor consequently any waves except such as are caused by the wind only, was, by the smoothness of its surface, as well as by the multitude of its islands, and the proximity of its neighboring shores, extremely favorable to the infant navigation of the world."[1]

A Mediterranean Sea in itself, the North Sea and the British Isles were crisscrossed by rivers, channels and canals, opening into the Atlantic to the west and penetrating deep through the Baltic passageway into Northern Europe—water made it possible for the fledging English industrial state to assemble a marketplace of vast intercontinental proportions. Says Adam Smith: "As by means of water-carriage a more extensive market is opened to every sort of industry than what land-carriage alone can afford it, so it is upon the sea-coast, and along the banks of navigable rivers, that industry of every kind naturally begins to subdivide and improve itself, and it is frequently not till a long time after that those improvements extend themselves to the inland parts of the country. A broad-wheeled wagon, attended by two men, and drawn by eight horses, in about six weeks' time carries and brings back between London and Edinburgh near four ton weight of goods. In about the same time a ship navigated by six or eight men, and sailing between the ports of London and Leith, frequently carries and brings back two hundred ton weight of goods. Six or eight men, therefore, by the help of water-carriage, can

< 96 >

carry and bring back in the same time the same quantity of goods between London and Edinburgh, as fifty broad-wheeled wagons, attended by a hundred men, and drawn by four hundred horses."[2]

Open sea navigation produced wealth only when connected to inland navigation—which was, in fact, the circulatory system carrying the life blood of the European economic organism. This was no secret to the pragmatic English, as Adam Smith attests so well, long before the grand theories of land-based Europe spelled out their dialectical magic. "Of all the countries on the coast of the Mediterranean Sea, Egypt seems to have been the first in which either agriculture or manufactures were cultivated and improved to any considerable degree. Upper Egypt extends itself nowhere above a few miles from the Nile, and in Lower Egypt that great river breaks itself into many different canals, which, with the assistance of a little art, seem to have afforded a communication by water-carriage, not only between all the great towns, but between all the considerable villages, and even to many farm-houses in the country; nearly in the same manner as the Rhine and the Maese do in Holland at present. The extent and easiness of this inland navigation was probably one of the principal causes of the early improvements in Egypt"[3]—he concluded, in a demonstration of English belief in the merits the pragmatic science.

93. Navigation and then trade, the emergence of a marketplace and demand for manufactured products, the invention of the separate condenser by James Watt, and the possibility of a textile industry, all these components made up the drive train of modern industrial civilization. That explanation is no longer just an ideological scheme, but the foundation of the mainstream

< 97 >

Western intellectual interpretation. The search for human factors, ideas, beliefs, or metaphysical insights has few adherents nowadays. To modern science, old time metaphysical arguments have no bearing in the workshop where industrial societies are forged.

One might stop to think of the workshop of the industrial mind itself, that made possible the creative act of technological progress. But that would be only a philosophical abstraction, of no interest to the men of industry themselves.

The Scholastic Mind's Industrial Revolution

94. Empiricism was, however, of interest to the scholars of the Scholastic debates, as early as the thirteenth century, when philosophy affirmed itself to Europe's higher minds as an independent science apart from theology and even dared to rise up against the latter. One of the first Schoolmen, John Duns Scotus of Dunston (a Scot from Northumberland) asserted that philosophy could acquire knowledge by natural means, leaving reason with no need for theology and its prescriptions for supernatural knowledge. This opinion started a long chain of developments in English philosophy, which for the first time acquired a voice of its own, and had far-reaching consequences for human history as a whole.

While he recognized the need for revelation, as a good son of his times, Duns Scotus also agreed with the

< 98 >

philosophic approach, against St. Augustine's view that man can know absolutely nothing of God without supernatural revelation. The philosophical view put rational knowledge of God at its center. Hence reason is man's highest authority, while the sacred texts have only a derived, conditional, and relative credibility that must conform to reason.

The contest between Franciscan Duns Scotus and his Scots friends, on the one side, against St. Augustine's party, now defended by Thomas Aquinas, on the other side, developed into a struggle between two powerful orders for Church supremacy. The early glory reflected upon the Franciscan order by St. Bonaventura was dimmed only by the fame of the Dominicans Albert the Great and Thomas Aquinas. In part jealous of the good name of the others' order, Duns Scotus endeavored to expose and refute what he called the errors of Thomism. Thomas, remaining true to the dogmatic and didactic tenets of the Dominican order, was the apostle of faith and grace. Duns Scotus, whose heart was filled with the spirit of the Franciscan order— spirit of living and practical piety—became the apostle of action, meritorious works, and human freedom. With an acumen wholly in keeping with his title, *doctor subtilis*, he undertook the criticism of St. Thomas.

The Thomist system bordered on pantheism, while the philosophy of Duns Scotus was decidedly Pelagian; in other words, the illustrious Dominican sacrificed the freedom of the individual to the great glory of God, while the Franciscan doctor believed that he was rendering God no less a service by exalting the individual and free-will at the expense of grace.

Thomistic determinism, assuming as it did the superior-

< 99 >

ity of the intellect over the will, struck to the core of Catholic philosophy. By bending the will beneath the yoke of an absolute principle, the Catholic fathers rejected the individual's self-love, took away his confidence in his own powers, and made him painfully conscious of his insignificance.

But when the foundations of such an all-enclosing system were tested they were found weak. On the one hand, it made God himself a relative being, whose will was subservient to his intelligence. On the other hand, it did more than humiliate the individual: it discouraged him and drove him to despair or to moral indifference. Should the Church adopt this system, it would soon cease to be the sanctuary of virtue and the mother of saints. Hence, in the view of Duns Scotus, the primacy of intelligence must be opposed by that of the will, and determinism must be substituted by the true philosophy and the real thought of Aristotle: the doctrine of divine and human liberty.

When Duns Scotus wrote these words he was barely thirty; he died at the age of thirty-four in 1308 after amassing writings that fill a dozen volumes. England at that time was just a far-flung insular country, semi-barbarian and totally unremarkable. Not yet a center of world trade, not a naval power, not a beacon of science or the site of any rare Rosetta stone; just a hilly country with a coarse life style, carving a living out of the harsh surroundings like the rest of forest-covered Europe.

Philosophy and religious questions were quite new subjects for this nation's mind, and few people had the luxury to explore metaphysical subtleties. One of Duns Scotus' few predecessors to deal with the themes of universal creation and pursue such abstract refinements

< 100 >

in a rational way was Scotus Erigena, a native of Ireland. He was the first great Schoolman.

While the object of philosophy was identical with that of religion, Scotus Erigena wrote, it studies, discusses and explains what religion merely adores: God, which is the universe. God is absolutely eternal, is immanent in the world, while every creature is virtually eternal only because our entire being is rooted in eternity; we have all pre-existed from eternity in the infinite series of causes which have produced us. The aim of human science is to know exactly how things spring from first causes, and how they are divided and subdivided. Science in this sense is called dialectics, which is not the product of imagination or capricious reason as the Sophists thought, but is grounded in the very nature of things.

Duns Scotus continued this elaboration along an even more independent line of reasoning:

If we would not confuse the true God with Fate or the *natura naturans* of the Neo-Platonists, he said, we cannot hold, with the Thomists, that the world is the necessary product of God's essence, his intelligence or his willpower. God created the world by an act of free will. It would have been possible for him not to create it. His will was not swayed by any higher principle, for it is itself the highest principle. The existence of the world, far from being necessary, is the effect of the free will of God.[4] Abelard was therefore wrong in assuming that God could create only what he created, and that what he created he created necessarily; and Thomas, too, was in error when he taught that the world was necessarily the best possible world. God did not create all that he can create; he created only what he desired to call into existence.

The logical consequences that followed are still with us today. Just listen to Duns Scotus's argument:

The first cause of things, divine will, is consequently also the supreme law of created spirits. Goodness, justice, and the moral law are absolute only insofar as they are willed by God; if they were absolute independently of the divine will, God's power would be limited by a law not depending on him, and he would no longer represent *the highest freedom or, consequently, would not be the Supreme Being*. In reality, therefore, the good is the good only because it is God's pleasure that it should be so.[5] God could, by virtue of his supreme liberty, supersede the moral law which now governs us by a new law, as he superseded the Mosaic law with that of the Gospel. In Creation, as in the government of the world thereafter, God knows no other law, no other rule, no other principle, than his own freedom.

Like God, man is free; the Fall did not deprive him of free-will. He has *formal* freedom, i.e., he may will or not will; and he has *material* freedom, i.e., he can will A or will B (indifference versus freedom of choice).

95. Though diametrically opposed to St. Augustine's doctrine, Duns Scotus' ideas were not disagreeable to the Church but were even encouraged for a time, as their danger was not at first apparent. By his emphatic affirmation of individual liberty, the subtle doctor proclaimed a new principle, an anti-authoritative principle. Elaborations of this principle grew from century to century and finally led to the emancipation of the religious consciousness. In a sense, Duns Scotus instigated the downfall of ecclesiastic tradition as the supreme

< 102 >

authority in matters of faith and conscience and, furthermore, opened the minds of his fellow men to a new focus. All his sympathies were, at heart, with the individual, for the will of the individual is his principle, and though he accepts that reason is common to all humans, he postulates the will as what characterizes the individual. The question of individuation became his favorite problem as this question would become the locus of later modernism.

His preoccupation with the issue of individualism defined Duns Scotus and set him apart from his contemporaries since all of them, including Henry Goethals and William of Champeaux, regarded the principle of individualism as a mere negation of authority and not a constructive affirmation of man's very nature.

Duns Scotus is, therefore, the first in modern times to declare individualism to be a positive principle. He gave it the name of *haecceitas*. The individual in this view is the sum of two equally positive and real principles: the *quidditas* (the universal, or the type common to the individuals of the same species) and the *haecceitas*, the principle of individuality or of the difference among individuals within the same species. The *quidditas* has no reality apart from the *haecceitas*, nor the *haecceitas* apart from the *quidditas*. Reality is found in the union of the two principles, of the ideal and the real—that is, in the individual.

96. Duns Scotus had broken the monolith of religion and dogma by rejecting so-called innate ideas and declaring, in *Questiones Subtilissimae*, that proof of the immortality of the soul and the existence of God are impossible from the standpoint of pure reason (science).

His first manifesto of individual liberty paved the way for the nominalism of his disciple Occam, whose doctrine of accidental creation produced the everlasting rupture between what we now call *science* and the authoritative rationalism of the Church. It advanced the modern method of empiricism. For, if the laws of nature and moral law itself were contingent, all sciences and morality depended on experience as their only basis. To place the will in the first rank in the book of metaphysics, and reason in the second, meant to subordinate reasoning to the methods of observation and experience.

In the late thirteenth century, a new school of thought sprung up on the soil of the English-speaking world. Its distinct voice would be articulated throughout the next centuries on a channel divergent from the still traditionalist, ruminating Europe and, finally, grow to full resonance on the world stage, almost four hundred years later, much to the surprise of the still medieval continental Europe.

97. William Occam, Francis Bacon, John Locke—the line of thought called English *empiricism* developed in complete divergence from the rest of the world. In relative isolation, the trickle down effect worked its way through the layers of society. The theory of causality and the methodology of observation and experience focused the energies of a whole nation, educated in that spirit formally and, even more so, informally. A national spirit, or what we call a *cultural constitution*—a national set of beliefs and an active methodology—was being spread, transmitted, developed, almost imperceptibly, from the highly learned circles, through imitation and contagion, through the lower middle class of traders, navigators and skilled workers. It grew into a *sui generis* book of national wisdom and truth.

< 104 >

98. What, then, triggered the novel approach of Duns Scotus? Was it some particular unknown characteristic of England alone?

The answer was given by Duns Scotus himself since, ultimately, the power and the will of creation, as he experienced it, was capable of generating, by itself alone, *being* under the lofty sign of liberty and individual self-consciousness. Like the forgotten principle of the *generatio spontanae*, human creation was to be understood as an act of self-determination. Duns Scotus was his own cause.

99. Anglo-Saxon by birth, Duns Scotus was the father of his nation through the Laws and the Commandments that he gave it. His wanderings through Oxford and Paris were his Egyptian wanderings. His Mt. Sinai was in Northumberland while his new nation was Britannia.

In the early 1600's Francis Bacon, loyal to his predecessors' experimental science, masterminded the continued unfolding of that quintessential English movement. An outspoken adversary of the metaphysical spirit, he expressly begs his readers to disparage any quest for abstract principles as worthless, commanding them "not to suppose that we are ambitious of founding any philosophical sect, like the ancient Greeks or some moderns; for neither is our intention, *nor do we think that peculiar abstract opinions on nature and the principles of things are of much importance to men's fortunes.*"[6] And so spoke John Locke, Isaac Newton and Charles Darwin.

The French drew their mindset from their own national ancestors, Thomas Aquinas, Descartes. The Germans had their Luther, and their Leibniz.

The story of Duns Scotus' individuality and the ensuing chapter in English history—the industrial revolution—is the *exemplary history*[7] that lies at the origins of our Western civilization. Our ancestor, he lives through his spiritual children as an invisible essence of what we are.

100. It is always possible to go farther back, to an originator older than the celebrated one. Moses himself might merely have collected the insights of his forerunners. Fathered and founded as a collective mindset, a nation is constituted as an entity of organic multi-body being, as a transcendent being—more than blood ties, common language, or territory—the embodiment of a higher level idea, belief, faith, value, understanding, viewpoint, creed, perception, trust, apprehension, principle, hope, conviction, sentiment and experience of life's meaning.

A nation's symbol and hero is reborn in every child. The hero is the model, the example, the norm, the inspiration by which the child sees meaning in his own life. Every newborn is to further, in measure with his own talent, the greater plan, the common aspiration that all share, carrying on his identity: to extend or at least maintain the glory, to defend the past, to attain the national purpose, to augment the original seed through his people, to prove the truth of the hero's prophecy. National epics, tales in the hero's name, the teaching of his views and, again and again, his method of action, are as much deliberately as forcefully embedded, inculcated, ingrained into the child. He is taught that it is patriotic to expound his ancestor's maxims, it is a duty to believe in what his parents believed, it is a matter of pride to obey their customs. A people is its collective identity.

< 106 >

101. That explains why in England, and nowhere else, a strange mania developed—this time, a grassroots aspiration for ingenious workmanship. A national fascination emerged with the practical, the empirical, and the examination of how things work. This evolved into a preoccupation with how improvements could be made to existing technology, how to succeed in industry, the trades, shipping and entrepreneurial achievement.

Something quite different emerged in neighboring Holland, which enjoyed about the same geo-economic circumstances. There, the national craze was painting. "As for the art of painting and the affection of the people for pictures, I think no other goes beyond them, there having been in this country many excellent men in that faculty, some at present, as Rembrandt, etc., all in general striving to adorn their houses, especially the outer or street room, with costly pieces, butchers and bakers not much inferior in their shops, which are fairly set forth; yea, many times blacksmiths, cobblers, etc., will have some picture or other notion, inclination and delight that the natives of this country have to paintings."[8]

Were English entrepreneurs more attuned to the comparative advantage that the industrial revolution would provide in world markets, inspiring them to become clever investors in the future, while the Dutch expended their talents and capital on bourgeois pleasures before they had a chance to capitalize on their fortunes?

One would rather conclude that English, Dutch, or Greek, they all, indeed, only attended to their innate visionary demands and to the natural imperatives of their congenitally bequeathed national mind.

A nation evolves as one original individual expanded into the larger human tribe. A people exists as a multitude of human beings, each one a potential new nation to come. Collections of many individual tribes, nations are *the one, the many and the all.* Thus, in a nation each element of the Trinity, in its own way, is present as the personification of the principles of *becoming.*

< 108 >

Notes

Chapter 1

[1] *Genesis* 47, 3, *Good News Bible (Today's English Version)*, (New York: American Bible Society, 1978).

[2] *Genesis* 47, 20-26.

[3] *Genesis* 47, 27.

[4] *Exodus* 1, 11.

[5] *Deuteronomy* 8, 7.

[6] *Deuteronomy* 6, 3.

[7] *Deuteronomy* 15, 6.

[8] *Deuteronomy* 28, 11-14.

[9] *Deuteronomy* 6, 4-5.

[10] *Deuteronomy* 18, 21-22.

[11] G. Vico, *The New Science* (Ithaca, NY: Cornell University Press, 1968), § 816.

[12] G.B. Vico, *The New Science,* § 768.

[13] *Ibid.*, § 779.

[14] *Matthew* 5, 17.

[15] *Mark* 7-7, 8.

[16] *Isaiah* 29-13: "The Lord said: 'These people claim to worship me, but their words are meaningless, and their hearts are somewhere else. Their religion is nothing but human rules and traditions, which they have simply memorized. So I will startle them with one *unexpected* blow after another. Those who are wise will turn out to be fools, and all their cleverness will be useless'."

Chapter 2

[1] Josephus, Ant. XIV, 8-10; cf. Suetonius, Caesar, 84.

[2] *Exodus* 21,1-12.

[3] *Deuteronomy 15,12-18.*

[4] Aristotle, *Politics,* 1253b33-1254a1.

[5] Aristotle, *Nichomachean Ethics,* Cambridge, 1934, 1172a35.

[6] *Deuteronomy, 11,13-17.*

[7] Aelian, *Varia Historia,* Leipzig, ed. M.R.Dilts, 1974 10.14.

[8] *Matthew, 23, 15.*

[9] *Nehemiah,* 13, 30.

[10] Plato, *Cratylus,* 402 B.

[11] Mullach, *Fragmenta phil. graec. ante Socrates,* Paris, 1860, pp. 101-102.

[12] Thucydides, Bk. III, ch. 82, in Toynbee, A study in History, (NY: Oxford University Press, 1987), p. 376.

[13] Seneca, *De Tranquillitate Animi,* in Dialogi. Selections (Warminster, Wilshire, England: Aris & Philips: 1994), pp. 61-65.

[14] Sextus Empiricus, *Adv. math,* VII, 111; Simplicius, *In phys.,* f. 7, 9, 19, 25, 38; Proclus, *Comment. in Plat. Timaeum,* p.

< 112 >

105, Clem. of Alex., *Strom.*, V., pp. 552 D, 614 A.

[15] *Matthew, 15, 1-9.*

[16] *Matthew, 18, 18.*

[16] *Deuteronomy,* 6, 4-5

[17] *Mark, 10, 27.*

[18] *Mark, 10, 29-30.*

[19] A.J. Toynbee, *A Study of History* (NY: Oxford University Press, 1987), p. 127.

Chapter 3

[1] Giambattista Vico, *The New Science*, § 1026.

[2] G. W. F. Hegel, *Encyclopedia*, § 50.

[3] G. W. F. Hegel, *Philosophy of Right*, § 273.

[4] We should have *idealists* for *realists* and *nominalists* standing for today's *materialists*. The latter emphasizes the real or material principles, which in the history of medieval philosophy represented Ionianism and Peripatetism, as distinguished from Academic idealism.

[5] In the Middle Ages the term *realist* meant *idealist*, that is, the direct opposite of what it means today.

[6] V.I. Lenin, *Materialism and Empiriocriticism*, (Bucharest: Editura Politica, 1974), p. 505.

[7] K. Marx, *For a Ruthless Criticism of Everything Existing*, in The Marx-Engels Reader (NY: W. W. Norton & Co., 1978), p. 13.

[8] K. Marx, *German Ideology*, in The Marx-Engels Reader (NY: W. W. Norton & Co., 1978), p. 248.

Chapter 4

[1] Adam Smith, *The Wealth of Nations* (NY: Penguin, 1987), p. 124.

[2] *Ibid.,* p. 122-23.

[3] *Ibid.,* p.124.

[4] Duns Scotus, *Magistrum sententiarum,* I., Distinction, 39, Question, 1.

[5] *Id.,* Distinction 44.

[6] Francis Bacon, *Novum Organum,* I., 116.

[7] Mircea Eliade, *The Sacred & the Profane. The Nature of Religion. The Significance of Religious Myth, Symbolism, and Ritual within Life and Culture* (NY: Harcourt Brace Jovanovich, 1959), p. 81.

[8] Jakob Rosenberg, Seymour Slive, and E.H. Ter Kuile, *Dutch Art and Architecture, 1600-1800* (1966), p. 9.

< 114 >

Index

< 118 >

Other books from Algora Publishing:

GRAND FORTUNES
Dynasties of Wealth in France

Going back for generations, the fortunes of great families consist of far more than money—they are also symbols of culture and social interaction. They are at the heart of dense family and extra-family networks, of international coalitions and divisions. The authors elucidate the machinery of accumulation and the paradoxically quasi-collective nature of private fortunes.

THE NEW COMMONWEALTH
From Bureaucratic Corporatism to
Socialist Capitalism

The notion of an elite-driven world wide perestroika has gained some credibility lately. The book examines in a historical perspective the most intriguing dialectic in the Soviet Union's "collapse" — from socialism to capitalism and back to socialist capitalism — and speculates on the global implications.

Ignacio Ramonet
THE GEOPOLITICS OF CHAOS
The author, Director of *Le Monde Diplomatique*, presents an original, discriminating and lucid political matrix for understanding what he calls the "current disorder of the world" in terms of Internationalization, Cyber-culture and Political Chaos.

Tzvetan Todorov
THE DEMOCRATIC PASSION
Benjamin Constant
The French Revolution rang the death knell not only for a form of society, but also for a way of feeling and of living; and it is still not clear as yet what did we gain from the changes.

Jean-Marie Abgrall
SOUL SNATCHERS: THE MECHANICS OF CULTS

Jean-Marie Abgrall, psychiatrist, criminologist, expert witness to the French Court of Appeals, and member of the Inter-Ministry Committee on Cults, is one of the experts most frequently consulted by the European judicial and legislative processes. The fruit of fifteen years of research, his book delivers the first methodical analysis of the sectarian phenomenon, decoding the mental manipulation on behalf of mystified observers as well as victims.

Jean-Jacques Rosa
THE EUROPEAN ERROR

Do we still have a choice? Here and there, the Euro is being adopted by governments, the media, and sometimes even by European citizens. They promise us less unemployment and more freedom. But are we so certain of the outcome?

Jean-Claude Guillebaud
THE TYRANNY OF PLEASURE

The ambition of the book is to pose clearly and without subterfuge the question of sexual morals -- that is, the place of the forbidden -- in a modern society. For almost a whole generation, we have lived in the illusion that this question had ceased to exist. Today the illusion is faded, but a strange and tumultuous distress replaces it. No longer knowing very clearly where we stand, our societies painfully seek answers between unacceptable alternatives: bold-faced permissiveness or nostalgic moralism.

Sophie Coignard
Marie-Thérèse Guichard

THE WELL CONNECTED
The Secret History of Networks of Influence

They were born in the same region, went to the same schools, fought the same fights and made the same mistakes in youth. They share the same morals, the same fantasies of success and the same taste for money. They act behind the scenes to help each other, boosting careers, monopolizing business and information, making money, conspiring and, why not, becoming Presidents!

Vladimir Plugin, Andrei Bogdanov and Vitali Sheremet
INTELLIGENCE HAS ALWAYS EXISTED

This collection contains the latest works by historians, investigating the most mysterious episodes from Russia's past. All essays are based on thorough studies of preserved documents. The book discusses the establishment of secret services in Kievan Rus, and describes heroes and systems of intelligence and counterintelligence in the 16th-17th centuries. Semen Maltsev, a diplomat of Ivan the Terrible's times is presented as well as the much publicised story of the abduction of "Princess Tarakanova".

< 122 >